You Can Work On-Camera!

Acting in Commercials and Corporate Films

John Leslie Wolfe
with
Brenna McDonough

D1073066

HEINEMANN
Portsmouth, NH

Heinemann
A division of Reed Elsevier Inc.
361 Hanover Street
Portsmouth, NH 03801–3912
http://www.heinemann.com

Offices and agents throughout the world

Library of Congress Cataloging-in-Publication Data
Wolfe, John Leslie.
    You can work on-camera! : acting in commercials and corporate films / John Leslie Wolfe & Brenna McDonough.
        p. cm.
    Includes bibliographical references.
    ISBN 0-325-00062-X
    1. Acting for television—Vocational guidance. 2. Television advertising. 3. Motion picture acting—Vocational guidance. 4. Industrial films. I. McDonough, Brenna. II. Title.
PN2055.W63 1998
791.45'028'023—dc21   98-27181
                                                                      CIP

Editor: Lisa A. Barnett
Production: Vicki Kasabian
Cover design: Darci Mehall
Manufacturing: Louise Richardson

Printed in the United States of America on acid-free paper
02 01 00 99 98 DA 1 2 3 4 5

Contents

Preface

This book is a practical guide for anyone who is interested in working in commercials and corporate films, and will apply, to some extent, to other television and feature film work. It doesn't matter if you are young or old, a professional actor or an amateur, we intend for *every single page* to give you specific information that you can use to audition for and to work in commercials and industrial films.

We use the term *actor* in referring to a person who acts, either male or female. *Producer* and *director* are also intended not to be gender-specific.

This is not theory. We are busy, working actors, and this is nuts-and-bolts, real information. It is what we learned *after* college. It's positive, a little Zen, and meant to encourage you. There is plenty to discourage you; we want to say, you *can* do this.

Dream big!

Acknowledgments

My thanks to my parents, Bill and Helen, who gifted me with their talents and their encouragement. To my children, Katherine and Aidan, who give me joy every day and who reawakened my imagination. To teachers and friends who have supported and nudged me forward. To Brenna, who loves and partners with me, and who helps me to believe in what I can't see. To my fellow actors, who inspire and teach me.

— John

First, I'd like to thank God. My mother, Jane, is a great source of daily inspiration. I am grateful to my siblings, departed and remaining, for their memories and sense of humor. Thanks especially to my sister Megon, who seems to be able to chronicle our life through music. To Mimi Doe, mentor and friend, who is always available to share her enthusiasm. To JoAnna Beckson, friend and teacher, another source of humor and inspiration available to me. To Dagmar Wittmer, for her great ideas. To Martha Royall, for her spirit. To all my agents through the years, especially my first, Shirley Hamilton in Chicago, who, when I said I was going to New York, lovingly said, "Don't come back!" To my children, Kate and Aidan, for their patience, humor, and wit. To my husband, John, for his love and dedication to our family and the craft of acting. Finally, to all the people who have crossed the On-Camera Training threshold. As they continually remind me, we are all students and teachers.

— Brenna

1

Introduction

As of this writing, a professional union-affiliated actor earns more than $500 per day, including pension and health benefits, for one day's work on a TV commercial or a "nonbroadcast" corporate film, and more than $800 per day for the "narration" on a corporate film. A *nonprofessional* actor on a nonunion job might earn half that, or even the same amount as a union actor, because some companies choose to remain nonunion, while still wanting to hire the best people.

Most of the fine universities with excellent theatre and musical training, including those that we attended, offer *no* specific training in working on-camera. Far more money is earned by actors working on-camera than by actors working on stage, and yet, to this day, I know many fine, working actors who say they don't know how to approach on-camera work or even what to expect at an audition.

With the basic skills that you are going to read about and learn from this book, we have trained actors, waiters, secretaries, lawyers, doctors, and many others who have gone on to work successfully in commercials, corporate videos, cable shows, and even television series work. The skills are simple to learn and, like so many things, require mostly a belief in yourself and the confidence that you gain from knowing what to expect and how the work is done.

Thousands of companies shoot "training films," better known as corporate or industrial films. Local and federal governments shoot these films constantly. As far as commercials are concerned, they are shot for everything, and they are shot everywhere, not just in New York City or Los Angeles. Thanks to the availability of good film equipment and editing facilities in so many cities, producers can shoot these jobs everywhere. Many large companies even have their own video/film departments. They depend on willing individuals who already work for their company, and on the talent pool in their area, to cast the many films they produce for training their people and selling their products.

1

There will always be room for the glamorous and beautiful people on the screen. But, the actors most in demand today are in the category known as "real people." Just turn on the television and watch commercials for a few minutes, and you will see. Most often, in corporate films and commercials, the actors are meant to portray the people who actually work at these companies, or who use the products — in other words, "real people."

Every day, new programs and channels are added to the ever-expanding cable TV system. The need for programming and talent is endless. Television advertising and video training are *essential* for the success of everything from business ventures to political campaigns.

So, whether you plan to keep working at your job with IBM, or you are just about to sign up for another year in the national tour of *Les Misérables,* or you are in the middle of acting school, there are enormous opportunities for anyone interested in working on-camera.

You can work on-camera. So, go to it! Earn some money, have some fun, and while you are at it, improve your communication skills and your confidence. Perhaps, even start a whole new career in acting, or expand on what you are already doing.

You can do it!

Acting Is Believing (or Don't "Act")

The formal study of acting, whether based on Stanislavsky or Meisner, can take you down many long and complex paths. Yet, a common and simple theme emerges from all training. Acting is believing.

For many actors, playing an ordinary person in a commercial or an office worker in a corporate film is much harder than playing Hamlet or Hedda Gabbler, even though the same acting skills are involved. Somehow, it's harder to play ourselves. Nonprofessional actors have an advantage here, because they haven't spent as much time learning to "act."

Ironically, children are very good actors. But, as we get older, we lose the natural ability we once had to pretend that we are a certain person in a certain situation. I think that it's mostly self-consciousness, imposed by societal expectations, that deprives us of our natural abilities as actors. *Self-consciousness is likely the single most difficult thing that you must conquer in your path to becoming a good actor.* This is true on-camera or before an audience. You can't concentrate on your work if you are worried about what others are thinking of you or of how they are judging you.

Another difficult thing for you to overcome will be your tendency to "act." The more acting training that you have had, the more you will feel the need to use it. But, to be a good on-camera actor, you need to be real; you need to be yourself. Which is simply to say, you have to think real thoughts and experience real emotions. That is what the camera sees. It sees thoughts.

Test the theory. Turn on the TV and turn off the sound. What do you watch? The eyes! Everything comes through the eyes. Unless the actors think real thoughts, the eyes are empty, no matter how much they are talking. But, if they are thinking real thoughts, feeling real feelings, you will get most of what is going on, even without hearing the dialogue.

So, one of your first tasks as an actor will always be to know what your characters are *really* saying—not just the words but how they feel about what they are saying and the situations in which they find themselves. Then you can concentrate on these real thoughts and deliver dialogue that is real.

Throughout the book, we will remind you, "Don't act!" If you feel that you are "acting," it's probably not good. You have to say real words like a real person, and think real thoughts.

If you think it, the camera will see it.

Acting is believing.

Your First Commercial Audition

When I went on my first "commercial" audition, I had already done three Broadway shows and I was, that night, to perform before a couple of thousand people in the national company of *Evita*. But I was a nervous wreck because I had no idea what to expect at a commercial audition.

Basically, if you have never experienced it, a commercial or industrial film audition goes like this.

1. You arrive at the casting office, sign in, and pick up a copy of the script for your audition, usually referred to as *copy*. There might

also be a "storyboard," which is basically a cartoon drawing of the scenes in the commercial. Industrial films or corporate films, whichever you choose to call them, will rarely have a storyboard.

2. You will study the copy and the storyboard for a few minutes, and when you are called, you will go into a room with a camera and stand on a mark on the floor. You will then be asked to "slate" (introduce yourself) to the camera, and perform the copy. They'll say "thank you," and then you'll sign out and leave.

3. Days later, you may be asked to repeat your audition at a callback. The one or two minutes that you spend in that room are where you land the job, or not. They are the source of great anxiety. However, you will be amazed and excited at how much you can put into those few minutes, and how you'll begin to look forward to them.

The audition should be looked at as a separate job altogether. Go to that job prepared and knowing what to expect, and not only will you lower your anxiety level but you can also have fun. So many actors dread the audition. But, the audition is your *opportunity*.

Always remember this. The casting people *want you to be good*. They have no investment in seeing you fail. They have a job to do: to cast this part. The better you are, the easier their job.

Concentrate on the audition itself, not on its outcome. There will probably be several people at your audition who could do the job, who give a great audition, but who don't get the part for one reason or another. Your job is to present your own unique self. The more that you can just relax and be yourself, the more successful your audition will be. Do that, and whether you get this particular job or not, they will call you back again for other things.

This is worth repeating. Don't worry about the results. No matter how much you might want this particular job, the less you think about the *outcome* as you are auditioning, the better your audition will be, and the better chance you will have to get the job.

Typecasting

An agent once said to me, "Know your type." Every casting call will include a description of the character they are casting. It might be as general as "mom," which implies a twenty- to forty-year old female. Or, it might be as specific as "male, African American, twenties, track star, open and friendly," which implies a young Carl Lewis.

Think of your "type" as one of your assets. If you fit the description of the character, typewise, then you are who they are looking for, so you are halfway there to getting the job. You can and should accentuate your type. Hairstyles and wardrobe are simple ways to help — something casual for a "mom," athletic wear for the "track star." Show up in a business suit and you probably won't make the callbacks for the mom or the track star.

Actors have a tendency to say "yes" to everything. I dare say, you could probably find a forty-year-old white guy, with a beer belly, who would say, "I can play that track star!" But, probably, it's wasted energy for him to try. If that same forty-year-old guy still wants to see himself as a college kid, he will miss all of the wonderful opportunities for his real type, the *father* of the college kid.

I have worn a hairpiece for work ever since I lost most of my own hair in my early twenties. Initially, the hair was good for my type, "all-American," later known as the famous "yuppie." Well, now that I'm in my late forties, I have an opportunity to play the "balding, real person," a very popular type right now. So, I shouldn't let my ego, or my mother's opinion of how handsome I look with my hair on, keep me from playing my real, and more marketable, type.

Of course, location will play a part here. My commercial agents in New York only want me without hair, because the "real person" is very big right now in that market. But, I also work frequently in the Washington, D.C., area. There, I mostly work in a suit and tie, and I wear the hairpiece, because that is the type that works there. So, I have separate photo headshots for each "look." I can't ask the casting person to make the leap of knowing what I would look like . . . if I looked different.

There are times when it gets silly, of course. Sitting in on a casting session, a friend of mine once heard a client say, after one actor's audition, "He would be *perfect*, if only he wore glasses." Now, most people have more imagination than that, but, if the casting description calls for glasses, you might have a pair of prop glasses handy, if you don't already wear glasses.

A realistic view of your type and the area in which you want to work will allow you to market yourself properly, and to compete in the category where you will get the most work. The good thing about typing is this. The "look" is so important that if you are the right type, you are already on your way to getting the job. You can forget about that aspect, and just concentrate on the work itself.

On the other hand, if they decide that they want a brunette, and you are a blond, you won't get the part. There is nothing personal in that. *You* weren't rejected personally. They just went with a brunette. Knowing there is nothing personal about their choices won't make you less disappointed if you don't get the job, but it should help lessen your anxiety going in.

It is also true that some casting people might like (or dislike) you because you remind them of an old girlfriend, or boyfriend, or cousin. They might like or dislike you for some minor, and seemingly fickle, detail. After I shot one commercial for a vitamin supplement, the director told me that I almost didn't get the job because the producer thought my sideburns weren't even.

The point is that you cannot control their perceptions. So, present yourself as well and as appropriately as you can, and then let go of the results. Concentrate on the work. If you are at the audition, they think you have the potential for the job. If you are at the audition, your chances are as good as everyone else's there.

Audition for Everything

Of course, the other side of physical typing is that it sometimes means nothing at all. Not long ago, Brenna, my wife and coauthor to this book, got a call to audition for an "infomercial" (a half-hour commercial that looks like a regular program). It was for a major theme park. The agent said that they wanted Willard Scott, the well-known television weather personality, or at least a Willard Scott *type*. Brenna's agent, however, had convinced them to see a few other people who weren't his type, and told Brenna to "just go anyway." Brenna got the job.

Brenna, of course, does not look at all like Mr. Scott. All of which is one more reason to let go of the outcome of your audition. If you get a chance to audition, don't concern yourself with whether you are right or wrong for the part. Just go and do your work. It is not up to you to do the casting, and every audition that you go on will make you better, more confident, more comfortable with auditioning. The more comfortable you are at the job of auditioning, the more you will be able to present that unique something that is you, and that is interesting.

I often hear actors say, "I hate auditioning!" But, it is the only process we have to get the job. So, let's accept it, embrace it even. An audition is an *opportunity*. If you are at the audition, you are in the running.

Attitude, Attitude, Attitude

Few things in life are not helped by a good attitude. In show business, not only does your attitude affect your business relations, it is also actually a part of your "product."

One of the wonderful things about this business is how much you can enjoy the work itself. Most of the actors I know, professional or amateur, pursue acting because they enjoy it, get pleasure from it, fulfill their passions with it. However, because there is so much competition, it is sometimes difficult to stay positive about the pursuit.

One of the best ways to stay positive and motivated is to do something for your acting career *every day*. It can be something simple: reading a trade paper, studying commercials that are on the air right now, reading out loud, making contact with an agent or a photographer. But stay involved so your interest doesn't atrophy.

You also have to surround yourself with positive people. Whether you're at an audition, working as an extra on a movie, or starring on Broadway, if you find yourself among a group of people who are just moaning and groaning about everything, don't take part. Leave, if you can. Those people are "energy vampires," and they will suck the enthusiasm right out of you. Besides, their experiences are not your experiences. You may get wonderful treatment from the exact person they are moaning about, and you can't allow them to color your perceptions or to give you their bad attitude.

Talent notwithstanding, wherever possible, people will choose to hire and work with actors who are pleasant to be around, who are productive, and who contribute. A positive work ethic will not only be appreciated, it will be remembered.

Agents and casting directors have long-standing, ongoing relationships. What you do at an audition or on a set—good or bad—gets discussed. Believe me.

One of the other aspects of attitude has a more immediate consequence: It affects your concentration. I am embarrassed to admit that I have, in the past, caught myself "thinking about lunch" while in a matinee of a long-running show. Not good! I got away with it, maybe, but only because the audience in a large theatre is a long ways away, and they had a lot to look at besides me.

But, cameras are usually just a few feet away. They see thoughts, and therefore, the lack of thoughts as well. If you are thinking about lunch, or about how you don't like the script, or about how you hate your hair today, that is exactly what the camera will see. A bad attitude will completely sabotage your ability to concentrate, to focus, and to do your best work.

Using a Video Camera

The single most important aspect of the classes we teach is that we videotape everything. When we play it back for the actor, we often ask, "How would you improve that?" Most of the time, the actor has a good sense of how to make it better.

Home video cameras are everywhere. As you consider the information in this book and as you practice auditioning, we strongly encourage you to get out your video camera (or borrow your neighbor's camera) and tape yourself. You will be amazed at what you learn from the playback.

You might even find a couple of like-minded people and work on some copy together. Even if they are not interested in becoming actors, this kind of exercise will help improve that "business presentation" that they have to make at work.

Learn from watching yourself on tape. Just be careful to not *criticize* yourself, or one another. At first, most people just look at things they don't like about themselves, like a mole or a crooked tooth. But your "flaws" are not what other people see.

The camera looks in your eyes; it sees what you are thinking and feeling. Evaluate yourself for whether or not you seem honest in your "performance." Were you believable? At some point, you will want to deal with your "look," the hairstyle and things like that. But, don't dwell on that now. You are the only one looking at that tooth you don't like. If you look for physical flaws on the actors in commercials, you will find plenty. But, unless you are an orthodontist or a plastic surgeon, their flaws will not be readily apparent to you when you watch their commercial.

Remember also that there is no "right" way to read a piece of copy or to play a part. Just read it your way. How many people have played Hamlet over the years? Although some were certainly better than others, probably none of them were the same. Your thoughts, your background, and your life experience all contribute to the unique way that you deliver a line.

In one class, when we were working on copy for a Caribbean cruise line, the actress decided that she would have the most fun by doing an "island" accent, wearing sunglasses, and dancing for the whole reading. Who knows if it would get her the job in real life, but it was fun to watch, and it was "her." The casting agent could always say, "We like that; now also give us a 'straight' one." Then she could tone it down a bit for the next reading. Trust your instincts. They will usually serve you very well.

Just keep in mind that with commercials and corporate films, the approach is nearly always *positive* and *upbeat*. The topics of corporate scripts are often rather dull, discussing office protocol, insurance benefits, or the best approach for dealing with customers and fellow workers. They hire actors to enliven the script, to make it seem more interesting.

As for commercials, turn on the television and try to find a commercial that does not have a positive message (with the exception of political spots, which we will discuss later). Even a commercial for a funeral home will try to leave you feeling good about their "product."

That is the purpose of a commercial; to make you desire the product, to make you want to buy it. So, as you watch yourself on the playback, also consider if someone else watching you would come away with a positive message.

Whatever camera setup you can find to use for practicing at home will be a benefit. It does not need to be high-tech. But, getting to see yourself, and *getting used to* seeing yourself objectively, will be a tremendous help to you.

Nervousness

Everyone gets nervous, even the people running your audition. If you weren't nervous, you couldn't do your best work. Stories abound about famous actors who, throughout their careers, would throw up before a performance. A fellow actor, whose father is a well-known opera tenor, once told me that sometimes before a performance his father would curl up on his dressing room floor in the fetal position, in terror about hitting the high "C" at that evening's performance. A big difference between professional performers and amateurs is not whether they *get* nervous, but what they do with those nerves.

First, appreciate the *need* for the adrenaline, produced by your nervousness, to bring you and your performance alive.

Second, disregard it. Don't announce to people, "I'm nervous." It won't be news to them, and probably, unless you announce it, they won't be conscious of it. Many young actors (I use the term *young* in reference to experience) are sure they could be seen shaking on their audition tape during the audition. As a result, that is all they could think about as they were auditioning. Playback of the tape only shows someone who is preoccupied with something. Most likely, only you can feel the vibrations of your nervousness.

This is another reason to audition and perform as often as possible. You will start to feel more comfortable each time — more able *not* to focus on your nerves.

Nervousness can cause your brain to "go to white," but it can also help you to focus and concentrate, to put an "edge" (in a good sense) on your performance. I've seen nervous actors who, when put in front of a camera, could not seem to remember even the simplest of things. I've also seen a nervous actor improvise an entire verse to a song, complete with rhyme, during the live performance of a show, when a fellow actor missed an entrance.

How do you control your nerves? You breathe and then breathe some more. You do your homework, so you know what you're doing. You realize that the people auditioning you are on your side. They may be munching on a sandwich or appear to be sleeping, but don't be fooled. They know that if they don't find someone good for the job, they may not get *their* next casting job. If you give a good audition, they look good for having you there. They *are* on your side.

Most of the directors that I have met genuinely like and admire actors, in part because of our willingness to go through the whole process of auditioning, for putting ourselves on the line.

Be nervous. It's OK! Use it.

Self-Consciousness

I believe that self-consciousness is the single biggest enemy of the actor. As you audition or perform, if you have any concern or thought about other people's opinion of you and your performance, then you aren't concentrating on your performance. You *have* to let go of other people's opinions, at least until later.

Self-consciousness comes in many forms. Sometimes it's an extension of your nervousness, but sometimes it's just a desire to look good, for the sake of ego. After all, appearance is a big part of the business. We spend years listening to parents, friends, and lovers coach us on how we look. Now (in a business where you are judged on how you appear), I ask you to forget other people's opinions?

That's what makes self-consciousness such a strong enemy. It is very difficult not to be aware of yourself. But, in watching actors rehearse over the years, I am certain that the best of them were willing to look absolutely foolish during their attempts to find good choices for the character.

Of course, commercials and corporate videos seldom require you to roll around on the floor, or look foolish. But the camera, staring at you as it does, exaggerates the sense that people are watching you. To a degree, your success as an actor actually depends on people watching you.

Regardless of the wonderful abilities to freely imagine and improvise that we possessed as children, most of us, around puberty, became very self-aware and are no longer able to lose ourselves in "play." The challenge we face as adults is to regain some of that freedom.

Finally, the most difficult form of self-consciousness to defeat comes not from others watching you, but from you watching yourself—

judging yourself as you audition and work, or even judging yourself as you just talk to someone.

We've all done it. "Talk, talk . . . ('I didn't say that line very well') talk, talk . . . ('Who wrote these dumb lines?') talk, talk . . . ('I hope I get this job') talk, talk . . . ('I hate my scene partner!')."

The casting agent responds with, "Thank you, Mr. Wolfe, who's next?"

Concentration requires focus. That means you have to think about *what* you are doing, not *how* you are doing it, or how you look while you are doing it.

This is not easy. It requires a certain leap of faith not to focus on the results of what you are doing. Self-consciousness is, in large part, an expression of your concern about the outcome of what you are doing. For a few minutes, forget your opinion of yourself, your opinion of what others think. You will love the results that come from true concentration, without self-consciousness.

Wake Up That Instrument

As an actor, your body and your voice are your "instruments." Speaking, singing, and acting are all physical activities (in come cases, athletic events). As you would for an athletic event, you should always warm up before you audition or work on-camera. Besides getting your instrument "in tune," warming up will release tension and reduce anxiety. Warming up gets your breathing going, improves your enunciation, sharpens your brain, and helps burn off some of the excess adrenaline that your body provides for you.

The mechanics of using your voice, simply put, involve pushing air through the vocal chords in a controlled fashion. A few sit-ups, panting (like a dog), specific vocal exercises . . . all are effective ways to get your voice and body warmed up. Stretching, to loosen up your muscles, will leave you more in control and more relaxed at the same time.

Warm up your face, especially your lips and tongue. A great thing to do is to read traffic signs and billboards, out loud and exaggerated, as you travel to your audition. Or, turn on some talk-radio station and repeat everything that is said. Again, really use your lips and tongue. If you are on the subway, read the advertising posters out loud.

Talking out loud as you walk or drive to your audition will cause some people to stare at you, but I've heard that it's a good way to keep from getting mugged. Seriously, people will look, but does it really matter to you? When you get to the audition, you'll have the confidence and ability that comes from a warmed-up, free, and loose "instrument."

Any of the traditional tongue twisters are also good for warming up your voice, or you can repeat some of our favorites. Start slowly and then speed up.

Exaggerate!

Some good ones include:

THE TIP OF THE TONGUE, THE LIPS AND THE TEETH.

RED LEATHER, YELLOW LEATHER, RED LEATHER, YELLOW LEATHER.

RUBBER BABY BUGGY BUMPERS.

CLIPPITY CLOP, CLIPPITY CLOP, CLIPPITY CLOP.

UNIQUE NEW YORK, UNIQUE NEW YORK, UNIQUE NEW YORK.

BIDDI, BIDDI, BIDDI, BIDDI, BIDDI BUM.

CAN YOU IMAGINE AN IMAGINARY MENAGERIE MANAGER, MANAGING AN IMAGINARY MENAGERIE?

You can also repeat the alphabet, very slowly, stretching your mouth widely on each letter. It all helps.

2

The Audition

In some ways, the audition is often more difficult than the job itself. So, master your audition skills, and you will do well at both the audition and the job.

First of all, *be on time* for your audition. It sounds obvious, I know, but the reasons are quite practical, and you would be surprised how many people come rushing in late.

If you are late, then you'll be under stress before you even start, so any nervousness you feel will be exacerbated. In addition, by being late you imply that you don't think this audition, or their time, is important. That's not a good way to start a job interview, which is what an audition is.

In addition, they may have planned for you to audition with a particular person. If you are late, you keep that person waiting, or more likely, they will move on, and you will miss the chance to be paired with the person they felt was ideal for you. If the commercial or film has several roles, they may audition in blocks of time for each character, so that everyone being considered for a certain role will be together on the tape. Arrive late, and you may not get to audition at all.

The earlier that you can get to an audition, the more time you will have to prepare with the script. We suggest you get there fifteen to thirty minutes early. One of my tricks, in fact, is to get there early and look at the copy before signing in. If the copy seems difficult, I slip out and spend a few minutes working on the script before I even sign in. That way, in case they are running ahead of schedule, I'm prepared. It does happen, sometimes, that you will sign in and the casting agent will say, "Come on in." However, if they do call you in early, and you are not yet ready, tell them you need a couple more minutes. As long as you arrived early, you don't have to feel rushed, no matter what happens.

When you get to the audition, it is also important to use well the time you have. Everyone loves to chat at the audition, to visit with friends, to "network," to meet new people, and to see what everyone else is doing. But, every minute you are chatting is time that you are not concentrating on what you are there to do. If someone wants to talk, tell them you'll meet them afterwards, or you'll go for coffee later.

A few actors will even subconsciously be trying to sabotage others by distracting them. Of course, there is always that one person who is completely negative, passing out "wisdom." You don't need it.

Say hello, excuse yourself, and then find a quiet corner to spend time on the script. If there is no corner, just ignore those around you and go to work. Don't worry that others will steal your interpretation of the script. They aren't you, and so anything they steal will have no effect on your audition. Don't be self-conscious about practicing in front of them. If they know what they are doing, they will be at work themselves, and they won't be worried about you. Of course, you do want to respect the other actors' needs for concentration, so work on your copy quietly, but read the words out loud. You won't know how they sound if you only say them in your mind. You need to actually say the words, so that your mouth has felt them coming out. In the audition, you can stumble over the simplest phrases if you haven't said them out loud.

It is in that waiting room that we all feel some of our most self-conscious moments, and where we do some of our best "acting" (acting like we're comfortable waiting there). But, at most auditions you'll have plenty to do while you wait. Study the copy, breathe deeply, meditate, relax, vocalize, breathe deeply. Mostly, don't worry. Eventually, you're going to have a lot of fun there.

The Copy

Most copy for on-camera work is divided down the middle of the page, with dialogue on the right side, and camera or scene directions on the left. If it is not in that form, it will be like a play, with the character's name and then the dialogue. If the copy for your audition is in the left-right, divided page form, be sure that you read both sides. You will often find valuable information about character or action on the left side that will influence how you handle the script.

Commercials are often made up with a group of vignettes, which are very short scenes with different people in different situations. The actor might have one line, or one word, or just a reaction. The audition for these will often involve some kind of improvisation or question-and-answer session, with no copy at all. We'll spend more time on that kind of audition later, in the section called "Reaction Shots."

Read the piece of copy you are given once through for meaning. Then, read it again, out loud. You have to get used to how the words feel in your mouth, their rhythm.

Have a pencil with you at your audition so you can mark the script to help you in your reading. You can invent your own method of marking, or use some of the markings that we will demonstrate. It doesn't matter what markings you use; the point is to remind yourself of choices that you made as you worked on the copy. When you get into the audition, and the adrenaline starts to flow, you won't remember how you wanted to say everything. Little marks to jog your memory will help you make the most of the time that you spent rehearsing.

Start with the punctuation that you want. For some reason, copywriters don't usually use much punctuation. Add commas where you want a little pause or lift, and exclamation marks where you want emphasis, and so on. You can also just use slash marks and underlining to show you where you want a pause or some emphasis. Those kinds of markings might catch your eye more readily in your audition.

Mark the key words and phrases, the ideas that are most important in each passage. Pay attention to thoughts that should be connected to one another, and connect them with a big arching mark.

Your commercial copy might end up looking something like Figure 2–1. (All copy is reprinted in Appendix A for you to mark up and play with.)

A piece of corporate copy might look like Figure 2–2.

You will probably find that corporate copy seems easier. Corporate scripts are often "slice-of-life," people having what might be a real conversation for the given situation. Commercial copy is compressed. It is like a small novel, a story with chapters, where you have to move from one emotion or thought to another in an instant.

These "chapters" are important to distinguish, because each one

> ... IT WAS REALLY T<u>OUGH</u> WHEN MOM PASSED
>
> AWAY, <u>DAD</u> WASN'T IN THE BEST OF HEALTH ...
>
> AND EVERYTHING FELL ON <u>MY</u> SHOULDERS./I'M
>
> REALLY THANKFUL THE FOLKS HERE AT THOMAS
>
> FUNERAL HOME WALKED ME THROUGH ALL THE
>
> *(smile)*
> ARRANGEMENTS ... STEP BY STEP./THEY EVEN
>
> CONVINCED ME NOT TO <u>SPEND</u> QUITE AS MUCH
>
> AS I WAS TEMPTED TO./
> *(slower)*
> <u>CALL</u> THEM ... THEY'LL TAKE THE TIME TO SEE
>
> TO YOUR NEEDS PERSONALLY.

Figure 2–1.

might need a change in rhythm or a different attack to make the transitions clear. The funeral home copy easily divides into three distinct "chapters," and each should get a slight shift in thought or energy (see Figure 2–3).

A corporate narration divided into "chapters" might look like Figure 2–4.

After a while, you won't feel the need to mark your scripts. But, you will always find it a valuable tool, and one that the best commercial actors rely on to help them put everything they can into the minute or two they have in front of the camera.

Scene 2 INT. FRANK'S CAR

FRANK drives with JANET, a computer specialist.
"friendly"

FRANK (Driving)

We'll be talking to Dan Whitney. He's the manager of the division that's developing the data processing software. They need actual tax returns and other documents for their computer programming prototypes. *(check mirror)*

JANET (Passenger)

Dan Whitney . . . What's he like?

FRANK *smile*

Young, intense, bright . . . he needs to be. Management gave him a tough job, overseeing the company's first government contract.

JANET

Does sound like a challenge . . . doing the startup and none of the employees have *Safedata* training yet. There's potential for a lot of disclosures.

FRANK

(A look) . . . If we do our job, that won't happen.

Figure 2–2.

(Chapter 1)

. . . IT WAS REALLY TOUGH WHEN MOM PASSED

AWAY . . . DAD WASN'T IN THE BEST OF HEALTH . . .

AND EVERYTHING FELL ON MY SHOULDERS. /

(Chapter 2) I'M REALLY THANKFUL THE FOLKS

HERE AT THOMAS FUNERAL HOME WALKED ME

THROUGH ALL THE ARRANGEMENTS . . . STEP BY

STEP. THEY EVEN CONVINCED ME NOT TO SPEND

AS MUCH AS I WAS TEMPTED TO. /(Chapter 3) CALL

THEM . . . THEY'LL TAKE THE TIME TO SEE TO

YOUR NEEDS PERSONALLY.

Figure 2–3.

Between the Lines

Commercials do more than tell stories; they also answer questions. (Of course, the underlying question is usually, "Why do I need this product?") Because of time compression, half of the conversation is often missing. Also, the action usually picks up in progress, so you miss whatever precedes the first spoken line.

In the margins, and between the lines, write things that fill in these gaps—things that help you make the lines sound more natural, more "yourself." You might write a suggestion of a physical movement or an

(Chapter 1)

MOST OF US ARE FAMILIAR WITH THE IMAGE OF A JURY DELIVERING A VERDICT. WE'VE SEEN IT ON TV SHOWS AND LEARNED ABOUT JURIES IN CIVICS LESSONS./(Chapter 2) IN THE NEXT FEW DAYS, YOU MAY BE DELIVERING A VERDICT IN A UNITED STATES DISTRICT COURT.

SERVING AS A JUROR IS ONE OF THE MOST IMPORTANT RESPONSIBILITIES YOU HAVE AS A CITIZEN OF THIS COUNTRY./(Chapter 3) THAT'S WHY WE'D LIKE TO TAKE A FEW MINUTES TO TELL YOU ABOUT YOUR ROLE AS A JUROR AND GIVE YOU A GENERAL IDEA OF WHAT TO EXPECT. ALONG THE WAY, WE'LL HEAR FROM SOME PEOPLE WHO HAVE ALREADY SERVED, AND GIVE YOU SOME DOS AND DON'TS ABOUT BEING A JUROR. SHOULD YOU BE SELECTED TO SERVE ON A JURY, THE JUDGE IN THE CASE WILL TELL YOU MORE SPECIFICALLY WHAT YOU CAN AND CANNOT DO. BE SURE TO ASK IF YOU HAVE ANY QUESTIONS.

Figure 2–4.

attitude that you think is appropriate for a certain line. You might write a question, the thought of which might cue your spoken line, such as "What does your product do?" or "How do you feel?" What you write doesn't have to be realistic or even sensible, but anything that you can add will energize your reading and make it more real. This "inner dialogue" will also help you with the pace of your reading (the tendency is almost always to read too fast) and help you get an inner life going for the camera to observe.

Figure 2–5 is a good example of commercial copy with clear little "chapters" and good opportunities for inner dialogue and emotional expression. Note where you can add smiles or laughs.

If all of this seems complex, take heart. It will get easier, and you will eventually be able to do most of the script markings mentally, but it is important to provide this inner dialogue. In real life, when you talk to people, you are constantly thinking about many things at once. You listen and have emotional responses to things they say, you think of what you want to say, and you think about the activity in which you are engaged. You do all of these things in every conversation, sometimes all at once. The more you can replicate this inner dialogue in your acting, the better actor you will be.

If all you do is say the words on the page, however beautifully, you probably will not get the job. You have to "tell a story."

Interpreting the Script

Often, clients will have only a general idea of what they are looking for in their choice of characters and interpretation for the script. You might get some hints of what they *think* they want by observing who is auditioning, paying attention to the general types that are there. Also, you will have heard or read a "breakdown" or description of the characters. The left side of the copy may also tell you something.

Beyond that, the script interpretation has to come from you and your life experience. Remember that there is no "right" way to deliver the lines. Each actor will have a unique way of reading the script, and your interpretation can be just as valid as any other actor's.

That said, it pays to observe certain things about scripts. The writers have worked for hours and gotten the approval of untold numbers of

(look up)

SOMETIMES A HEADACHE AT NIGHT WILL GET

ME SO TENSE, THAT BETWEEN THE PAIN, AND

("I admit")

THE TENSION, I JUST CAN'T SLEEP! ENOUGH

TO MAKE IT HARD TO LOOK GOOD THE NEXT

(smile)

MORNING. BUT THERE'S A PAIN RELIEVER THAT'S

MADE FOR NIGHTTIME HEADACHES . . . EXTRA

(relief)

STRENGTH PM. IT RELIEVES THE HEADACHE

AND ITS TENSION, AND GIVES YOU EXTRA HELP

TO RELAX, FOR A GOOD NIGHT'S SLEEP, . . . SO

(smile)   (lean in)

YOU SHOULD WAKE UP FEELING FINE. TRY EXTRA

STRENGTH PM. . . . 'CAUSE IN THE MORNING,

YOU MAY ONLY LOOK AS GOOD AS YOU FEEL. !

Figure 2–5.

people before you ever read the lines. In the case of commercials, the script has probably been analyzed by the company's legal department as well.

If, for example, a word or phrase is repeated, then you need to make something of that. If you find words that have an obvious connotation or feeling, make that a part of your reading, and mark the script to remind yourself.

Consider this opening to a cruise line commercial:

IMAGINE THE EXCITEMENT OF VISITING THE SEAPORTS OF SPANISH PIRATES . . . IMAGINE WALKING ON COBBLESTONE STREETS OVER FOUR HUNDRED YEARS OLD . . . IMAGINE LUXURIOUS, DUTY-FREE SHOPPING, AND MILES OF SILKY WHITE-SAND BEACHES . . .

Imagine begins the first three sentences. Clearly, the writer intends for you to make use of that word in several ways. Words such as *luxurious* and *silky* offer great connotation. These are words that are meant to create visual images.

Think of how these words might sound if this spot were on the radio and you had no pictures. You need to make just as much of the words for television. Even though they will probably show beautiful photographic images in the commercial, your narrative should enhance the images and stimulate the viewer's imagination.

Of course, at the audition, there will be no beautiful photographic images, so you have to provide them from your mind and with your words. You have to make the client see the images.

Find the words in the script that you can use to create the pictures. Let your eyes twinkle, and let the excitement be heard in your voice when you say "Spanish pirates . . . cobblestone streets . . . shopping . . . white-sand beaches." Picture your own reaction to seeing these things, and let the excitement show in your voice. (You will find much more about this in the section called "Visualizing.")

Another thing that is *very* important! Read all of the parts as you study the script. There are two reasons. First, perhaps the most important thing you do as an actor is to *listen* to the other characters so your responses to those characters are appropriate and, more basically, so you say your lines on cue. Therefore, you have to know what the other characters say.

The second reason is that, very frequently, after you read the part you were brought in for, the director or casting agent will decide to have you read one of the other parts. They switch people around all the time once they see them standing there.

It's great when that happens because you get considered for more than one part. So, you want to be prepared by having read all of the parts in advance.

Smile

Everyone enjoys seeing other people smile, and there is evidence to suggest that smiling and laughing actually improve your health. You probably even know that smiling is easier than frowning, that it takes fewer muscles.

It seems ironic then that smiling on-camera is so difficult for people. Yet nothing you do will contribute more to your effectiveness as an actor in commercials, corporate films, and even voiceover work, as smiling. Play a role on a television crime drama and your smile might not come into play at all. But try to sell a product on a commercial, or warm up a dull script about insurance benefits for a company, and it will be your smile that invites the audience to watch you, makes them comfortable with you, expresses your confidence, and helps them to like and accept you and your product.

Take a few minutes to watch commercials on TV. Watch only to observe the actors and their smiles. How many commercials do you see in which the actors are not smiling full-time?

Friends of yours may describe you as "perky" or "joyful," and you may think it an odd notion for me to suggest that you might have difficulty with smiling on-camera. Your first few times in front of a camera, you will probably think that you are smiling the whole time. But, if you get to see playback, you will be surprised to see that you did not smile nearly as much as you thought.

This is a great exercise for your home video camera. Take a piece of copy, from this book or elsewhere, and practice reading it for the camera, concentrating just on smiling.

Smiling takes some effort. We usually only smile in response to something pleasant or funny, so you have to plan to smile, to rehearse it into your script.

Write it on your script: *smile,* or *warm it up,* or even *laugh.* A very small laugh is very effective, and something you will hear used all the time with voiceover work, especially. But, whether you are on-camera or doing the voiceover, the only way that you can look or sound warm, perky, friendly, or happy is to physically smile.

If you don't consider yourself a particularly joyful person, then spend some time practicing your smile. Practice it while looking in the mirror. Practice belly laughing until a smile just lives on your face. Dig into your "sense memory" to remember a moment that truly made you smile or laugh. Recall that moment for inspiration, or put on some comedy album that really makes you laugh, and get used to how a smile feels.

If you are aware that your smile is crooked, or that you tend to smile to one side in a sort of half smile, then spend some time in the mirror exercising a good, full, even grin. Muscles control your smile. You have to train the muscles by using them, and like any exercise, the more you do it, the easier it becomes. Eventually, a smile will come very easily to you.

Many people are self-conscious about smiling because they think that they don't have a good smile. But, for the vast majority of people, the only thing wrong with their smile is that they don't use it. A smile is infectious; it makes you and the people watching you happier just doing it.

If the importance of smiling is the only thing that you take away from this book, your money will have been well spent, because a smile will get you jobs. I suppose it is true with success in other pursuits as well, but with on-camera work it is an absolute reality — a smile will get you jobs.

So . . . Smile!

Political Spots

There are some serious commercials, certainly, in which the smile comes only from the announcer or from the actor during the tag end of the spot to finish it on a positive note. Commercials for legal services and public service announcements (PSAs) come to mind, and, certainly, you will find many corporate films with a serious message. I did one, for instance, about employee theft in a large supermarket chain.

One category of commercials, however, is actually negative more and more often: political spots! Among the most popular of them is the vignette-style "testimonial," in which the "regular American Joe/guy next door" (played by a professional actor, of course) decries the way this politician, or that new law, or these regulations are ruining our lives and fouling up the country.

Evidently, to advertise that the other guy is bad is more effective than to advertise that your guy is good. So, the negative political ads are here to stay, at least as long as they work.

Try these samples. The names have been changed to protect . . . well, you know.

AS A PARENT I'M CONCERNED ABOUT WHAT KIND OF PEOPLE LEAD OUR COMMUNITY. CALL ME OLD-FASHIONED, BUT CHARACTER MATTERS TO ME. AND THAT'S WHY I HAVE SOME REAL QUESTIONS ABOUT ANDY PARKER. IT SAYS RIGHT HERE THAT PARKER WAS THE SUBJECT OF THREE SEPARATE INVESTIGATIONS INVOLVING LAND FRAUD. AND PARKER REFUSES TO EXPLAIN THE OFFICIAL COURT RECORDS SHOWING HE DIDN'T PAY CHILD SUP-PORT . . . IS THIS THE KIND OF PERSON WE WANT REPRE-SENTING OUR VIEWS . . . AND OUR VALUES?

Here is another example:

BY NOW YOU'VE HEARD ALL THE ARGUMENTS FOR AND AGAINST THE NEW FUEL TAX. IF YOU'RE STILL UNDECIDED, HERE'S SOMETHING YOU MAY WANT TO KNOW.

THE PEOPLE SUPPORTING THE FUEL TAX SAY THEY NEED THE MONEY TO REPAIR UNSAFE BRIDGES AND CONSTRUCT NEW ROADS. THAT SOUNDS GOOD, BUT UNFORTUNATELY, IT'S NOT COMPLETELY TRUE.

FIRST OF ALL, THEY DON'T NEED THE MONEY. THE STATE HAS A 170 MILLION DOLLAR REVENUE SURPLUS FROM LAST YEAR, AND THE POLITICIANS BEHIND THIS TAX DON'T TELL YOU THAT NEXT YEAR, THEY HAVE THE POWER TO TAKE THIS MONEY AWAY FROM ROADS AND PUT IT INTO THE GENERAL FUND, WHERE THEY CAN SPEND IT ANY WAY THEY WANT.

PLEASE DON'T BE INFLUENCED OR MANIPULATED BY MISLEADING EMOTIONAL APPEALS. THIS TAX IS NOT IN YOUR BEST INTEREST. I HOPE YOU'LL JOIN ME IN VOTING AGAINST THE NEW FUEL TAX.

As negative as these spots seem, you still need to find places to lighten them, to be pleasant, even if you don't actually smile. With this Fuel Tax copy, you might deliver the first line with an "understanding smile" in your voice, and the last line as warm and friendly as you can. Of course, take your cues from the director or casting person, but lightening some of the lines will add dimension and interest to your delivery.

Rehearsal

You are at the audition, you've picked up the copy, and you've read it. If you know that you are paired with someone or are in a specific group, ask them if they would like to rehearse the scene. They might be reluctant, from self-consciousness, but most people will work with you if asked.

I can't overemphasize the advantage of rehearsing. Even if you don't know who you will be partnered with, try to read the scene with someone there. Find a corner and do it quietly, if need be, but rehearse it out loud, just as you do when you are reading by yourself.

Block the scene, in a general fashion, so that you and the other actors are in agreement as to how you might relate to one another physically, or where to visualize something that is referred to in the copy. You may get some direction once you go into the audition, but you will read better if you are not trying to invent direction as you go along. It can be very distracting to be auditioning and suddenly realize that you and the other actors are pointing to something in all different directions.

The more that you rehearse the scene, by yourself or with others, the more in control and confident you will be inside. Don't worry about other actors watching you or stealing your interpretation. Your exact interpretation will look and sound different with someone else doing it. Don't let their watching intimidate you. (Besides, they are probably using the waiting room to chat and catch up on old times. You are preparing.)

We do not recommend that you try to memorize the copy. With only a few minutes to prepare, trying to memorize the copy will cause you to concentrate only on that. Your interpretation will go right out the window, and usually the only thing that shows on your face is an expression of you trying to think of your next line.

Instead, do the best you can to memorize the first and last lines of the script, so you can deliver them with good eye contact to the camera. Keep the copy chest high and in line with the camera, so that you only have to drop your eyes to pick up your next line.

Now, if you get the copy far enough in advance, or only have a line or two, then by all means memorize it. Anything you do that will increase your ability to have eye contact with the camera or with the people for whom you are auditioning will increase your chances for success.

Once you get into the audition, the director or casting person may ask you if you want to run it once before they tape it. The correct answer is *always* yes. If they don't offer, you can ask to rehearse it once to get familiar with the room. Almost everyone gives a better reading the second time through, so if the first time was a run through, the real one will be the better reading. Just remember, they want you to give your best audition as much as you do, and they will accommodate you to the extent that time permits.

At many auditions, the copy will be printed on a large white card located near the camera lens. Once you go in, start reading the copy out loud as soon as you get to your mark, while they are focusing the camera or adjusting things. The copy on the white card will often be slightly different than the page you got outside, and the words will be in a different placement. If there is more than one character, the lines will probably be color coded.

If the person running the audition says "ready?" and you haven't gotten all the way through the card, ask to be allowed to read the rest of the card. Don't take forever, but don't feel rushed either. The cards are great for getting the copy out of your hands and improving eye contact, but they can foul you up if you try to read them "cold," even if you really did a good job learning the copy from the printed page before you came in. The words just look different on that card, so you have to get familiar with them as they appear on the card.

You may find that when you get to the audition there are no scripted lines. But you will still see a storyboard or get some information on your character and the circumstances or the setting. You should still rehearse before you go in. Plan a couple of things that you might do or say, appropriate to what you know so far. "Write" a line or two for yourself to have ready for your "improvisation." (See the section called "Reaction Shots" for specifics.) *The less you have to think on your feet in the audition, the more relaxed you will be and the better you will audition.*

Props and Wardrobe

Wardrobe and props can be very effective for suggesting a character or circumstance. However, *suggesting* is the correct word. The casting agent will not enjoy your showing up with a suitcase full of costumes and props.

Actors are fond of saying that casting agents have no imaginations. But, if you look at things from their point of view, they shouldn't have to imagine how you could look if you looked different. Their job is to assemble some actors who are appropriate, who have the basic abilities to play a certain part, and then to audition them and find who (they hope) is the right person for the job.

You must do what you can to serve the basic vision of the character. If it is a doctor, a business suit would be fine. But, if you had a lab coat that you could wear over a dress shirt or blouse, with a couple of pens in the pockets, that would be a simple way to suggest the character. You don't need—and you should not bring—full surgical gowns, blood pressure machines, and X-ray films, even if you own them.

On the other hand, wearing jeans and a workshirt would not only keep them from seeing you as a doctor, it would probably keep you from being able to play one, because of differences in body language that you would adopt wearing the more casual clothing.

A pair of sunglasses for that cruise ship ad could be a nice touch; just don't keep your eyes covered. Wear them in your hair, or put them on at the end of your reading, as a tag. An engineer might have a few pens in the pocket; a carpenter might have a pencil over one ear. Simple, realistic things can work nicely for you by suggesting the character and even perhaps giving you an activity during the reading.

Don't spend a lot of time, however, looking for ways to prop a scene.

It doesn't add that much, and it could distract you. For instance, starting the dialogue as you take a sip from a cup of coffee could be very realistic, but, if you are stuck with the cup in your hand for the rest of the audition, you would not be helped at all.

This is a case for following your instinct. If you have an instinct to use something, then do it. Just think through how you would use it, and how you would get rid of it.

The great thing about simple props is that they help to keep you honest as an actor. Most of the common props that you might choose you will have used in real life a thousand times. So, your body will move and react in a natural and realistic fashion. But, it is important that if you ever use a prop, you *really use it*. People always look at their watch to show impatience, or to show that they are in a hurry. But, if you choose to do that, actually read the time, or it will look fake and unreal, which will hurt your acting rather than help it. If you choose to drink from a cup, really put your mouth to the lip of the cup and drink. Pretending to drink with a real cup looks fake and makes you look fake as an actor, so we don't believe you are drinking and we don't believe what you are saying.

Of course, once you book the job, you will be using lots of props and wardrobe. We discuss props and their continuity of use in Chapter 7 "The Job."

Just remember, in some ways you will have more on your mind at the audition than at the job, and you will be less prepared. Therefore, add only props and wardrobe that *help* you, without getting in your way.

Direction

When you enter the audition room, there will be brief introductions of the people there. Generally, you are not well served by a lot of conversation here. Brief, cordial greetings are fine. Just be yourself (the pleasant part of yourself) and then *listen*.

It is during this moment, after you say hello to everyone, that you will get whatever direction you are going to get. With all that you are thinking about at that moment (the script, your nerves, who are all these people, did you put money in the meter? etc.), it is easy not really to hear what the director might say. But, tell yourself to listen.

Keep in mind that your audition begins the moment that you step into the audition room. Your body language, your confidence, your lack of confidence, your attention, your lack of attention . . . all of these things go into the little mental computers of the casting people to allow them to form a first impression of you and of how it might be to work with you.

Once introductions are made, some directors will ask you to run the piece once to get a sense of how you are approaching it. They may then give you some direction, ask you to run it again, and then tape it. If that happens, great. Just as often, you will get no direction whatsoever, because they don't know how they plan to shoot it, or because they want to see your ideas, or because they are not the actual director.

Some directors will have you do it once and then give you directions for doing it in some completely different way. Often, they're not challenging your choices; they are interested and want to see if you can take direction. It's sort of a little test. But, it makes sense for them to do this, because the client or ad agency may be giving them lots of ideas on how to shoot this piece, and the director needs to know if you listen and if you have some flexibility. Again, listening is your first job.

If you only have one line or phrase, casting people are very fond of saying, "Just give me three different readings." For instance, your line might be, "IF YOU DON'T GET IT, YOU DON'T GET IT," meaning "if you don't buy the product, you must not understand." This would be a perfect situation for them to ask you for three different versions.

Try that line a few different ways. If you have your camera nearby, record them, and see if they are really different. They are probably not as different as you thought they were.

When you do a line different ways, the idea is not to just say the words differently, but to have different attitudes. So, choose three *specific* attitudes. Happy, curious, silly, calm, intelligent, sad, amazed . . . pick three of these, or three of your own. Read the line with the specific attitude in mind, and you will see great differences.

Try the same thing with the following lines:

"NOW THIS, THIS IS GREAT GUM."
"IT STOPS MY PAIN, IT HELPS ME SLEEP."

"IT'S 100% JUICE."

"I'LL BET YOU CAN'T EAT JUST ONE."

These are examples of lines I read at auditions or heard on various commercials. You can pick others. The point is to try each line with different attitudes. One-liners like these can be more difficult in an audition because you have to direct yourself. So, anytime you see just one line on the page at an audition, get at least three versions (attitudes) ready before you go in.

Whatever direction you get at an audition, probably the one that most actors get most often is "Slow it down." The actor's tendency is to rush, to speak too fast. We all do it at some time. Your adrenaline and excitement level will always make you want to rush. So, if it seems like you are speaking unnaturally slow, then, probably, you are at the right speed.

In the classes that we teach, at our own auditions, and in performance, we constantly have to remind our students and ourselves to "Slow it down."

The Slate

"Hello, I'm John Leslie Wolfe."

Whenever you audition on-camera (and this should include when you practice on your own camera), you will be asked to "slate" your name at the beginning. If they want any other information (your agent's name, your age) they will tell you.

Think of the slate as your "handshake" with the camera, and your "handshake" with whoever views that tape. The slate is about *you*. It is separate from the copy that you will perform. In that brief moment the client can and should get a sense of who you are. Is your "handshake" confident, relaxed, excitable, bored, apologetic? Be aware of the message that you are sending. Practice it at home looking in a mirror, or on your home camera.

Good! Now, add a smile to it.

After you slate, take a moment and collect yourself to move your concentration to the copy. Most actors feel rushed at that moment.

They say their name and then rush into the copy. Don't. Make yourself take a full two or three seconds to make the shift from the introduction into the performance.

At first, you'll feel embarrassed about not speaking instantly after your slate. But remember, this is your audition, your time. Whether the audition takes one minute or ten, those minutes are yours, and you owe it to yourself to make the most of them. Rushing yourself won't make the most of your time. You are not wasting the casting people's time by taking a moment to focus, especially if that moment of concentration helps you to do a better audition. Slate, take a moment, then begin.

Once in a while, you will have an audition where they will ask you to slate and then to talk a little about yourself. Some jobs involve no script; they might just have a generic action (maybe you're the person admiring that new car). So, the director may want to get to know you a bit. It is important to remember that directors are not testing your skills as a scriptwriter. You don't have to be funny, or entertain the room. They want you to talk about yourself, things you have done, things that are important to you. Reciting your credits tells them a little about you, the person. They might ask for some of your resumè, but more than likely they just want to get a sense of who you are. Of course, if being funny *is* you, then entertain away.

I have seen this technique of having actors talk about themselves used for a Broadway musical audition as well as for a commercial audition. And I have seen fine, experienced actors who, at a party, could entertain people for hours, freeze up entirely when asked to talk about themselves at an audition. Keep in mind that the director just wants to get a feeling of who you are, what it would be like to be around you, what kind of attitude you have, what got you to that audition.

Sometimes, as a part of your slate, you will be asked to give them a left and right profile. If they do call for that, then after your say your name, turn ninety degrees to one side, hold for a second, turn back to camera, then turn ninety degrees to the other side, hold for a second, and return to facing the camera. They want to see how you look from different angles, so don't move too fast.

At the end of your audition, the casting person will occasionally ask you to "tail slate," or "end slate." In that case, they want you to repeat the same slate at the end of your audition as you gave at the beginning. This allows the clients to be reminded of who you are, without rewinding the tape, when they are reviewing the auditions.

Working with Other Actors

If you meet the actor(s) with whom you will audition and rehearse before going in, you are already ahead. Once in the audition, rehearse together again in front of the camera, if at all possible. You'll be able to smooth out any physical activities, adjust your reading to that space, and unload some of your nervous energy.

Commercials and corporate films are message oriented. They don't take much time for exposition and character development. Therefore, much of what the audience learns about you will come strictly from how you relate to one another physically.

At the audition, you may need to be instantly "familiar" with the other actors. You might need to touch or put your arm around someone whom you have never met. Here again, rehearsing is important. You can tell that person that you might want to hug them, or whatever you plan to do, at this or that point in the script. The more comfortable you are relating to one another physically in the audition, the more successful you will be in telling the story of who these characters are.

If you are working with children, it is particularly important to let them know if you plan to touch them or hug them. Otherwise, they most likely will not "play along."

In real life, we allow a little space between ourselves and others—the less we know the person, the larger the space. But, the image in a camera is two-dimensional and has varying perspectives, depending on the focal length of the lens. The camera compresses things in such a way that in order to look normal, you often need to be closer to other people than you would naturally be. It takes a little getting used to, but don't let it make you feel uncomfortable. Invariably, the person running the camera will ask you to "squeeze together" if you are in a group. Three "business" people, dressed in suits in a corporate video, might have to sit knee to knee in order to look natural on the screen. If you are standing next to others, you will be shoulder to shoulder. Flip on the

34

TV and look how close people are to one another, and yet how it looks normal. But, it does feel a little strange in auditions.

As is true in real life, the most important aspect of working and communicating with others is listening. Regardless of how much or how little training we have had as actors, it never hurts to be reminded of that. Acting is, in large part, a matter of reacting to a situation or to what someone says. You might someday get to play a great monologue like General Patton's flag speech in the movie *Patton,* or the St. Crispin's Day speech from Shakespeare's *Henry V.* Mostly, however, you will have dialogue — conversations. With conversations, whether in life or in acting, effective communication starts with hearing what the other person says.

Beyond that fact, the most interesting shots, in feature films and corporate films alike, are often the shots of a character listening. Those shots produce or heighten the dramatic effect. We don't know if something a character says is good or bad, except by watching another character as he or she hears the news. Even news interview shows like *Dateline* or *48 Hours* are using the "listening" shot more and more to lend dramatic effect and interest to a story. So, being a good listener will not only improve your acting by allowing you to react more honestly, it will also get you more time on-screen.

In an audition situation, you haven't had the script very long, and so you naturally focus on your own lines. However, since you know that the other actors' lines are cues for yours, your tendency will be to follow their lines on the page to watch for your cue, without actually hearing what they say. Often what happens is that you speak, then your eyes go to the cue card or page you are holding to follow the other lines, you speak, your eyes go, etc. The effect of this on the tape is that you completely drop out of the scene when you are not speaking. So, no matter how well you deliver your own lines, you don't seem to be a part of the scene.

Rehearsing with someone before you audition will help get you off the page. The main thing to get is the idea of what the other characters say, and learn the last two or three words that are your actual cue. Then listen. You will learn tricks over time, and it is easier if there is a cue card, because you can glance away in a natural listening reflex and sneak a peek at the card. Just don't lock your eyes on the card. If you are holding the script, keep it high and in a position so that you can glance down with your eyes, with a minimum of shifting yourself out of a listening position. You can look at the script as though you are reflecting on what the others are saying, or as if you are thinking about your response.

Listening is a very active process. Watch people in real life and on television. When they listen, they aren't just staring at the other person. They move, they think, they look around, they shake their heads, they smile, they frown. All of these are possibilities for you as you "listen" to the other actors with whom you are working. As a practical matter, within these moves you can find places to check in with the script.

When you are working with another actor or in a group, it is what you do when you are *not* speaking that helps to make you seem real and believable.

Mistakes

Whether you are just starting out or have twenty years in the business, you will make mistakes. Of course, on the job they'll just shoot it over (which they will probably do even if you are perfect). But, part of the reason that auditions seem so much harder than the job is that not only are you less prepared, but also it feels like you only have one shot at it.

Just keep in mind that this is *your* audition, and you are in control of it. If you make a mistake, the best thing you can do is to ignore it and go on. If you feel that you can't go on, then stop and pick up where you made the error, or tell them, "I'd like to start again."

Do not apologize. Making a mistake is nothing that you have to feel "sorry" for. Taking a mistake in stride and not letting it throw you off is a sign of your confidence. Just stop, collect yourself, and then go on.

If you are in the middle of your audition and something goes wrong or you make a mistake, and you feel that the whole thing is just going downhill, then do not continue. It will only get worse. In reality, a mistake you make might be small or even imperceptible to those watching, but if it throws you off to the point that you can't recover your concentration, then you should stop and do it over. Of course, you can't do this over and over, but it's a rare casting person that won't understand and let you do it over again. Many casting people edit the tape down before they show it to the client anyway, and they will get rid of your bad take. Remember, they *want* you to be good. How would it serve them not to let you do a better take?

On the other hand, I can recall making a mistake on a reading and when I asked the casting director if I should do it over, she told me she liked the first one. She thought the mistake made it more real. The main thing is not to let a mistake add to your stress. We have all given bad auditions in which we made no mistakes whatsoever. A *good* audition won't be ruined by a mistake unless you make a big deal out of it.

There is one type of "mistake" that can work both for you and against you: paraphrasing. You are in the middle of your audition, you have looked away from the script, but you know the meaning of what the script says, so you change a couple of words. This is perfectly fine to do. If, however, you paraphrase too much of the script, you can get lost, and you begin digging a hole that just gets deeper and deeper. If that happens, stop and get back to the script.

On a shoot for an industrial film, the client or director may even encourage you to put some things in your own words, to help make the script more conversational. However, when shooting a television commercial for a product, you'll have to say what is written, because the script has been cleared through the manufacturer's and the advertising agency's legal department. Unless the legal department is represented on the set and is willing to approve a change, you will have to stick to the script, exactly.

In the audition, if you do paraphrase, some directors will ask you for another take with the script as it is written, just to make sure that you can do it. I have worked with a couple of actors who had memory problems; they just couldn't retain the words on the page. If that happens on the set, it can eat up a lot of expensive time, and a director doesn't want those kinds of problems.

You also do not want to imply, with too much paraphrasing, that you don't care for their script. Very often, the director for an industrial film is also the author of the script. They tend to like their own words — a lot — and they want to hear them spoken.

Basically, as for mistakes, you treat the audition and the job differently. In either situation, fewer mistakes will boost your confidence and your concentration, and the goal should be to make as few mistakes as possible. But, accept the fact that you are going to make mistakes, and don't let them undermine the work that you are doing.

At an audition, that means doing the best you can to ignore it and move on. At a job, it means fixing the problem as efficiently as possible, so *they* can move on. That may mean you have to write words you are forgetting on a prop that you are holding, or ask the actor to whom you are speaking (and who is off-camera) to hold the script up for you. There are lots of ways to help yourself on a set, and we will deal with more of these tricks in Chapter 7, "The Job."

Reaction Shots

We have talked about camera shots of you listening. The extension of that is the "reaction shot," a shot of you responding to a situation or stimulus without using any dialogue. Someone says something to you, we see you hear it, and then we see how you feel about what was said.

The importance of listening shots and reaction shots can't be overstated; often it is that shot that provides the meaning for the scene for the audience. For instance, a man in a film scene says to a woman, "I'm going to pick up your daughter after school." That line by itself means nothing until we see the woman's reaction. Her reaction — glad, relieved, fearful, anxious, or whatever it may be — tells the audience what is going on in this scene. It tells us if he is a bad man or a good man.

This is a great opportunity for an inexperienced actor to display his or her lack of experience. The tendency is usually to overact. Without the benefit of words, most people will want to use their faces, and that is the trap. The thing that you do not want to do is to "make faces."

The camera sees thoughts. For a reaction shot to be good, it has to be honest. It's as hard and as simple as this: think the thought, and your eyes and face will contribute the appropriate expression all on their own.

Now, certainly there are some people, with a comic flair, who have rubber faces and can make great, expressive, silly expressions. If a director does ask you for silly faces, and you have that ability, then "mug" away. There are certainly television commercials where the actor does just that. But, usually, you will need to decide what *specific* thought or

38

emotion it is that you want to express, and then let us see you experience that thought or emotion mentally.

In a formal acting class, you will spend, or you have already spent, time working with concepts like "sense memory," where you recall specific events in your own life that generated the emotion that you now want to portray. You try to remember how this event made you feel— how it affected you physically and emotionally.

Let's say that you want to express fear. You were mugged once, and you truly felt fearful at the time. You concentrate on the memory of that event to regenerate the physical manifestations you had at the time. Once you become skilled at this exercise, you get to where you can recall the feelings by themselves. Simply put, you are now using sense memory.

Commercials and corporate films will rarely ask you to portray dark, complex emotions. They are overwhelmingly upbeat. Your task, therefore, will be somewhat simpler. Smile, and generally you'll look happy, whereas in order to look sad, you can't just frown. But, the principles of honesty in your expression remains the same, and the smile is only real if it's in your eyes. That means actually feeling happy.

The best way for you to generate an honest reaction shot is to write a script for yourself. Write what you might say if you could use words to express what you are being asked to say without words. Then, as you mentally recite this inner dialogue, your face and body will supply the needed expressions.

For instance, let's say you are in a car spot. The director says that he wants lots of excitement from you as you, the customer, look at the car. So, you write a script. "What a *great* car! I love this car! Man, I'll bet this thing goes fast! Wouldn't I look great driving this? Oh boy, the kids would have fun back there! Oh, look at that stereo!"

You invent, and then actually say to yourself, lines such as those, and your body will do the right thing. As long as they keep the camera rolling, you just keep improvising *specific* internal dialogue, and your face and body will keep reacting properly.

If a director asks you for a big smile, then you mentally say to yourself something like, "That is *wonderful!*" Then the smile will be in your eyes as well as on your face. It will be real.

It may not still be running when you read this book, but for some time Cheer laundry detergent has had on the air a wonderful series of spots with a terrific character actor, a bald man, usually in a bow tie. Without any dialogue whatsoever, he shows you some dirty pieces of laundry, something that would obviously be a challenge for any detergent. He lets you know how he feels about these laundry messes, then pours some Cheer on one, and pours Brand X on the other. Then he just swishes them around in bowls. The filthy thing washed in Cheer becomes wonderfully clean, and the actor shows it off with his own subtle version of pride. Of course, the other brand didn't do so well. They shot several versions of this spot, some without even using Brand X, and some to show how the colors stay bright with Cheer. As you watch the actor's deadpan delivery, you can imagine an entire story and conversation. Each commercial is a wonderful series of reaction shots, with all sorts of opinions and emotions expressed by the actor, without his saying a single word out loud.

Most likely, a basic story line was provided in storyboard form to the actor, and he and the director probably worked through a scenario. Maybe his inner script starts off with, "Oh, here's something. Yuuuck! Who did this? What do you think, can anything get this clean? Maaaaybe!"

We use this commercial as a basis for an exercise in class to work on reaction shots. You can use it with your camera, or just in a mirror.

Get two pieces of fabric, or two socks, or two anything. Look straight at the camera, lift the two things up to either side of your face, and look at each one (out of the corner of your eye). Let us know that you think they are bad, or even hopeless. Then, put them down, and pick them up again to show us how one of them is now clean and lovely, while the other one is a disappointment. End it with a reaction to the good one.

Think specific thoughts; don't make faces. When you watch the replay of yourself, watch only to see if you believe what you are saying with your eyes and face. Don't worry about whether the expressions on your face are funny or ugly or dumb. Are they believable? You'll know whether they are or not.

Try another exercise, on your home camera if possible, or in a mirror. (If you use a mirror, be sure you think honest thoughts, and use the mirror just to observe what happens to your face as a result of those thoughts. A mirror will tempt almost any actor to make faces rather than thinking real thoughts.)

Now, get some things that actually smell really bad and some that actually smell really good. Smell the real thing and react honestly, good and bad. Now, use something that has no actual smell at all, and replicate the thought, feeling, and reaction that you had to the real things, good and bad.

If you audition for a commercial in which you are to taste something, most likely the casting people will hand you something like a clean plastic spoon and tell you what kind of reaction they want to see. You'll do the rest. Give yourself specific inner thoughts. Don't play the "reaction" that they ask for (good, bad, etc.); play a thought that *causes* that reaction. Even though you aren't using words, your job is still to "tell a story."

Tasting shots are often done either profile or three-quarter profile, so that the product doesn't obscure the actor's face and reactions. You might want to audition that way as well.

Whatever reactions you choose to portray, be careful about scrunching your face up or knitting your brow to express your feelings. It closes your eyes, and basically it is not very attractive. You can express the same feelings by opening your face up (lifting your eyebrows instead of knitting them), and it lets us see a brighter and more expressive face.

When you do a job that has no scripted words, it will often be shot "MOS." This is a term romantically attributed to an early German director who would say that he was shooting "Mitt-out sound!" Others have attributed the origin of the phrase, less romantically, to a more technical explanation of "minus optical strip," the optical strip being the thin strip along the edge of motion picture film that contains the audio information (which includes dialogue) for playback. I prefer the "German" explanation, but in either case, it means the same thing. No sound is being recorded to go along with the image. If there is a microphone anywhere near you, it won't be turned on.

MOS exercises are valuable tools for sharpening your storytelling skills. If you do not have any dialogue, you are forced to involve your imagination more fully. The goal is not to turn you into a good pantomime artist. Instead, we want you to improve your ability to visualize and tell the story. Where are you? Who else is there? What are you doing just before and just after you speak your lines?

Of course, at some point, you might have an MOS audition. MOS or any improvisation exercises that you do will help prepare you for an MOS audition, but more important, they help make you a better storyteller when you have dialogue. (See Appendix B for MOS exercises.)

Your Friend, The Camera

Put a camera in front of most people, and there are two very common reactions. Either they become rigid and clam up, or they get silly and act completely goofy. We have all seen the self-parody of home movies, and seen our friends or family members act in ways completely unfamiliar to us. Strangely, the ubiquitous presence of cameras in our lives has not changed their ability to make us self-conscious.

In our classes, a major goal is to have the students spend enough time in front of a camera so that it takes on less importance. That is one purpose of suggesting that, as you read this book, you work with a video camera, whenever possible. The goal is for you to think of the camera as merely a companion in the room, or even better, as a friend.

Good camera acting requires that you be simple, subtle, and natural. Although I risk sounding like Harold Hill in *The Music Man* (who proposes the "think system" for learning to play a band instrument), the best way to convey a thought to a camera is to actually think the thought.

When I began auditioning for commercials, I was working on a Broadway stage at night. I was doing theatre. I saw the camera lens as a window through which I should perform to this great large audience. I was wrong.

You will hear actors discuss the "size" of their performance as they compare stage and camera acting. As a practical matter, camera acting must usually be "smaller," because the audience (the camera) is not as far away. But, the correct way for you to think is not in terms of size, but in terms of honesty. It is the stage actor who is acting in an unnatural, and often dishonest, way when he or she creates some oversized and dramatic gesture so that it will "play to the back of the house." When I learned to act on-camera, to convey thoughts honestly, to act with my eyes and not my arms, I became a better stage actor as well.

What is different from real life, when you are acting on-camera, is visual perception. That has to do with why you have to "squeeze in," or cheat your face around, or otherwise adjust your physicality. Think of it this way. If you are standing twelve inches from someone and the camera records you from a great distance, then you will look very close together, because of all the space around you in the frame. But, if you are twelve inches apart and the camera records you in a close-up, with no space around you at all, then the visual perception is that you are not particularly close to one another.

The visual perceptions are affected by things like the focal length of the lens, but unless you are particularly interested, you don't really need to know the physics. You need to know how the scene is being shot—close-up, head and shoulders, group shot—so that you can be as physical as would be natural, given that visual perception. In a close-up you would want to move very little. Indeed, anything that you did with your hands would likely not even be seen. In a group shot, even though you might be standing closer to the other actors than what feels natural, your physical gestures should be of a size normal and honest to the given situation, and real in terms of who you are addressing.

If you are addressing the camera, you speak to the camera as if it were a person standing where the camera is standing. Sometimes, the camera will be set up at a distance with a telephoto lens so they can capture scenery and then zoom in on you for your dialogue. In that case, you still play the camera as though it were just a few feet away. You will probably be wearing a radio mike, so you will still be able to achieve the same intimacy of talking to a "person" directly in front of you.

The most effective way to bring intimacy and a personal quality to your performance in front of a camera is to imagine the camera to be an actual person. Again, the more specific you can be, the better. My wife always imagines the camera to be either the woman who is her best friend, or her sister. I usually imagine the camera to be my father, or my wife, or a certain friend, depending on the product or situation.

If you are playing a group scene, you will usually avoid any awareness of the camera, except in one sense. The camera has to see your face. If you are talking to someone in profile, "cheat" your face toward the camera, or find ways to turn in the direction of the camera as often as possible. We will discuss this more later, in terms of hairstyles and other things that block the camera's view of your face, but just know that if you can't see the camera, it can't see you.

When you are speaking directly to camera, talk to a real person. Look into the lens in the same way that you would look into a person's eyes when you speak to them. Don't just speak in the direction of the camera. If you prefer a specific focal point, then look at the top edge of the lens.

To help with this concept of personalizing the camera, try this exercise. Set up your camera, or something that represents a camera. Get some practice copy, either from this book or from a good magazine ad. Decide who you want the camera to be (your friend Martha, for instance) and write that friend's name at the front of the copy. Then deliver the copy, "MARTHA, IMAGINE THE EXCITEMENT . . ."

Then, practice delivering the copy without saying the person's name out loud, but continue to say it to yourself just before you begin speaking out loud. This is a good way to put a real face on the camera, and personalize your reading. The camera is your friend.

After the Audition

Someone says "cut" and your audition ends. Invariably, however, there is a brief second or two after the last word you speak or action you perform, when you feel you are finished but no one has said "cut." The audition is still going on. When you finish the script, just hold. Hold the last thought or expression your character was playing, or just smile into the lens. Until the casting person has said "cut," or you are absolutely sure that the camera has stopped rolling, do not leave, look away, or otherwise comment on your audition.

If the audition is an improvisation, you might do well to invent an action or a line of dialogue to "tag" the scene. That puts a positive ending on the audition, and lets them know you are finished. But even so, don't break the moment on your own.

You may have thought that you didn't do as well as you could have, or you may just be glad that it's over. The casting people may have loved you, but as soon as you roll your eyes or frown, they will change their minds and agree with your opinion. It is a terrible thing to do to yourself. Reviewing an audition, hardly anyone thinks they were perfect and most of us can think of things we could improve. However, I can honestly say that as far as my on-camera career goes, I have never seen any relationship between my opinion of an audition and whether or not I book that job. That is not true for theatre auditions. There, sometimes you know. But for on-camera, you just don't know what they see or what they are looking for. The only *sure* way to have them not take you seriously is to negatively comment on yourself at the end of your audition.

Sometimes, the casting people will continue to "roll tape" for what feels like a long time. They might be zooming in to get a nice close-up of you, or they might just want to give the client a nice long look at you. Just smile and hold, hold, hold. If you think that you could have been better, keep it to yourself, because *they* might think that you have just the quality they are looking for.

When you finish and leave, it's a good idea to have a plan for the rest of your day. We tend to put a lot of importance on auditions. When they're over, it is very easy to feel let down, just from the drop in adrenaline if nothing else. It's very easy to move into the "How did I do?" phase.

You can replay the audition over and over in your mind, and you probably will. But, it's not very useful. If there are general things about your technique that you want to think about and fix, fine. But replaying an audition over and over in your mind will only serve to frustrate you.

Move on. Go back to your other job. Meet a friend for coffee. Wash the car. Always have a plan before you go to your audition for what you will do after. If you accept the fact that working in this business is something that you are going to do, then auditioning is just a part of your day. Obsessing about the results just exaggerates the importance of the audition, which makes the next one harder. You will still do it, of course, but go easy on yourself, because you have very little control over the outcome.

Usually, the casting people will show the audition tapes to the client(s) from the company or organization sponsoring the job, and everyone who gets a vote will voice their opinion about who they want. You will be talked about in great detail. (I mentioned earlier that one client thought my sideburns were not even.)

After whatever process they use to narrow the choices, they will usually then "callback" a few people. Sometimes they callback everyone; sometimes they callback just one person. Once in a while, they book from the first audition tape. But, in the larger markets, such as New York City and Los Angeles, it is very unusual.

If you get a callback to audition again, they will sometimes ask you to change something or add something to what you did the first time. If they call you back and they tell you *nothing,* the conventional wisdom is to do exactly what you did the first time. They called you back because they liked what you did. So, don't change it unless they ask you to. It is a good idea to write, in your appointment book, notes about what you wore and what you did at an audition. Sometimes, the callback audition is days or even weeks later, and you might have forgotten the specifics.

Everyone has their own opinion on this, but we usually do not recommend calling the casting agent to find out how you did. You can call your talent agent, if one represented you, to see if *they* got any feedback. Of course, in cities other than New York and Los Angeles, the casting agent and the talent agent are sometimes the same person.

As a way to follow up after an audition or meeting, we usually suggest things like sending a note to thank them for calling you, and asking them to "keep you in mind." Do not send them two dozen roses. Agents have told me that actors have done that, and the agents found it embarrassing, which actually hurt the actor's chances of being called again.

Later on, after you have been doing this for a while, you won't need to do anything to follow up, but, until you feel established, a little gracious reminder now and then won't hurt.

3

Zen and You

Recently, as a student was walking up to do her piece in class, she made the comment that she was very nervous. We explored it. I asked if she was afraid that we would judge her. She said she was afraid she would "fail." We told her that she couldn't fail, because there was no right or wrong way to do it, just her way. Well, she took that message to heart, and on her next take, she added a flamenco dance to her reading, a completely individual way of approaching the copy, and one that was delightful to watch.

Most people have heard of, if not read, the books on "Zen and the Art of . . ." There are variations on the theme. It is fairly well accepted that some professions require a person to be not just talented, but also to "believe" he or she can accomplish the job. Professional golfers and pitchers come to mind. In one style of archery, referred to as "bare bow," the archer does not actually aim the bow. Instead the archer focuses all concentration on the target and visualizes the arrow hitting the center. It is a very accurate style of archery.

The concept of "thinking" or "believing" your way to success is not unfamiliar. But few people apply the concept to themselves. We want to convince you that being a little "Zen" can serve you in powerful ways in your pursuit of on-camera work, which in turn will open you up in other ways you don't now suspect.

The *American Heritage Dictionary* (1989) defines Zen as "A school of Buddhism that asserts that enlightenment can be attained through meditation, self-contemplation, and intuition rather than through the scriptures." We are not suggesting Buddhism or any other religion for you. We are suggesting that good technique, proper theory, and good training are not enough in pursuing on-camera work. Maybe, they are not even that important. The people who achieve the greatest suc-cess—who get the most out of their pursuit—not only in their work but also in other areas of their lives, all reach a little further, all are a little "Zen."

So, we will say things to you like "You are equal to thé work that is expected of you" and "Dream big." We believe it, and we believe that no matter the degree to which you end up pursuing an on-camera career, you will benefit from opening yourself to these ideas.

Open a door for someone, and a door will be opened for you. It's true, literally. Hold a door for someone, and in that moment you will have a communication with that other person. Ours is a business of communication. Good communication must be a part of your life. Also, in our business, you will depend on "networking" to learn things about the business — about projects that are coming up, good photographers, the name of a new agent, and on and on. Open doors for one another, and make new friends in the process.

Give freely of your time and talent. Volunteer to read at your local Books for the Blind or at a retirement home. It improves your communication skills, it helps you practice expressing yourself, it opens you. Giving of your time takes you outside of yourself and gives you perspective. You will meet people who can teach you and help you, and you'll feel the pride and confidence that comes from helping them.

We want you to feel open to possibilities — to the possibility of your success.

Meditation

To many people, meditation has taken on more of a connotative meaning than a literal one. Images of sitting cross-legged with candles burning and New Age music playing come to mind. Most of us have felt unqualified and unable to enter the mystic world of meditation.

But in fact, meditation has a fairly simple definition: "to reflect upon, to contemplate." It is simple, but it has been found by many to be a powerful tool for focusing concentration, for calming oneself in a high-energy world. Candles and music enhance the experience for some people by helping them to shut out some of the outside world and to relax.

You may feel tempted to move on to the next chapter now to avoid indulging in any "hocus-pocus." But there is no magic involved, no religious theme — and you don't even need to believe in meditation to do it. Just do it as an exercise. You can take a few seconds or a few minutes. You don't have to tell anyone about it; just read on and try it.

Turn off the TV and any other random noise generators, sit comfortably, and just read this next paragraph. You can read it a few times, if you like.

> At this moment, I am exactly where I am supposed to be. I am ready to experience new things. I am calm. I am ready to do something good for me. Today, I will compliment another person and will accept, without argument, every compliment given to me. I am equal to the job I have ahead. Nothing and no one can come between me and my greatest good.

We program our subconscious mind with our conscious thoughts. For some reason, it seems easier to reach for the negative than the positive, so we say to ourselves, "I can't do it" or "I'll never make it." If we see an obstacle, we tell ourselves, "I can't get around that."

The biggest part of a coach's job is to motivate the players, to make them believe that they can swim a little faster, run a little harder. People hire personal trainers to tell them, "Come on! You can do it. Give me one more!"

The subconscious mind will take what it hears, from your coach or from you, and go about making it happen. So, it is possible, even if you don't "believe," that you can make something happen just by hearing it enough times that you become convinced.

It is said that we use only 10 percent of our brains. If that is true, then think about how much you can accomplish by tapping into and programming a little of that unused part.

Here is a list of words, all of which have various rich and connotative meanings for different people. Pick one, at random, and just concentrate on its meaning to you. Think about how it applies to you, about how you can include more of it in your daily life. Then mark this page, and come back to it every now and then to choose another word, and spend a minute or two. Incorporate the positive aspects of words like these into your thoughts on a conscious level, and they will find their own way into your subconscious.

Patience	Gratitude	Strength
Power	Integrity	Joy
Truth	Courage	Expectancy
Simplicity	Balance	Creativity
Abundance	Humor	Efficiency
Trust	Flexibility	Openness
Harmony	Grace	Responsibility
Faith	Adventure	Freedom
Purpose	Honesty	Play

Working as an actor requires you to explore and express a greater range of emotions and sensations than most jobs. Working as an actor requires you to constantly motivate yourself. Positive thinking, meditation, and affirmation are tools of the trade — tools that you can use every day.

We are creatures of habit, and we tend to forget or postpone things that are not a part of our routine. So, think about a point during the day when you could take a moment of quiet time for yourself, and put it on your schedule for the next thirty days. For me, mornings are a good time because the usual demands of the day have not yet begun to distract me. Choose a time that is good for you, but make it around the same time each day so you don't forget or postpone it. Think of this as a time just for you, a time to focus on your intentions, on your career (goals), on your life, and on those who share it.

Begin your meditation (quiet time) by the simple act of breathing freely and fully, getting in touch with the life force coursing through you. Clear your mind, and find yourself in a comfortable position, feet flat on the ground, spine straight, head held comfortably, eyes open or closed. You should be in a quiet location, without distractions. Again, this can be just a couple of minutes a day. It shouldn't disrupt your day or take a lot of planning. Think of it as a gift to yourself.

If you feel uninspired, or just for the sake of variety, choose a word from our list and consider it as it relates to you and your life, or choose one of the "meditations" we have printed here.

Here are a couple more meditations for you to choose from and read. From time to time, pick one out and read it, out loud if possible. You can program yourself for success and exercise your speaking muscles at the same time.

This is the beginning of an exciting time. There are many opportunities ahead of me, and I am equal to the challenge those opportunities will provide. I will focus on what *has* come my way, rather than on what has *not*, and I will remember not to make the project more important than myself. I will face challenges, knowing that within me is the ability and knowledge I need.

What I need to succeed, I already have.

Meditations needn't be complex or time-consuming. This simple phrase can easily be memorized and repeated just before an important audition or meeting.

I go forward with trust and excitement. I am confident and calm.

No matter how much you know, there are those who know more, from whom you can learn, and those who know less, whom you can teach. Seek, and accept, any positive affirmation you can find that supports what you want to achieve.

Breathing

Wherever you are right now, sit down, and take seven breaths, very slow, very deep. Use your entire lungs.

How do you feel? Calmer? More aware? What else?

Nothing we consciously do is more important, and more taken for granted, than breathing. If you sing or do yoga then you have already spent time learning breath control. The greatest value that breathing will have to you as an actor (other than the obvious concepts of enabling you to speak and stay alive) is in your preparation.

Pressure and anxiety cause you to shorten your breathing. But you can lessen that anxiety and get yourself more in control with slow, deep breathing. It will also help you to focus your thoughts and energy.

Before you go in for your audition, as you sit in the waiting room (with a lot of other actors who are trying not to look anxious), consciously slow and deepen your breath. You will feel less nervous, more focused, more confident. Your voice will be more steady and lower pitched, which, even if you don't feel it, makes you seem confident and sure.

On the set, as you are trying to concentrate on what you say and do, people will be all around you, adjusting lights, fussing with the microphone that's hidden in your clothing, brushing powder on your face, and giving you direction (all at the same time). The best thing you can do to block out all the distraction, to focus your concentration, and to stay relaxed, is to breathe deeply.

Breathing is a muscular event, entirely controlled by the muscles in your abdomen. You will hear people speak of breathing with the diaphragm, which is the muscular membrane that separates the internal organs of your chest and abdomen, but that is misleading. In reality, you use all of the muscles from your pelvis up to your chest and all the way around into your back for breathing. To control your breathing, you need to train and exercise those muscles.

First, however, you need to make a mental connection with how your breathing works. The day that I was on my way to becoming a real singer was the day my junior high school choir director (God bless him, wherever he is) got me in front of the choir and showed me this connection. This is how he did it.

Picture yourself at "the big game." You shout "Hey!" like you are yelling to someone down on the field. Go ahead, try it. It needs to be a short, explosive-sounding "Hey!" What part of your body moved? Your chest? No, your stomach, or diaphragm, if you want to call it that. Notice how powerful and loud a sound you can make using those abdominal muscles rather than your chest muscles. Yet in most people's minds, deep breathing will mean heaving their chest up and down.

Women, especially, tend to breathe with their chest, probably because of their clothing and what they are taught about good posture. Men probably tend to be less concerned about letting their bellies expand. Controlled breathing means expanding and contracting your belly.

Belly breathing also allows you to take deeper breaths. Try this. Take as big a breath as you can, expanding only your chest. Now, let your belly expand, all the way down to your pelvis, and you will be able to take in maybe 20 percent additional air.

As a commercial or film actor, you'll probably never have to sing an aria on-camera, so you can be less concerned with the mechanics as long as you learn the basic benefits of good, deep breathing. It will calm you, give you more mental and physical control, and focus your thoughts.

I was reminded of this recently when I was waiting to audition with an actor who is a familiar face on movie screens. While everyone chatted around him he put his hands in his lap, closed his eyes, and started breathing in long, slow, deep breaths.

I copied him.

Visualizing

If you are reading this book, then you have already begun to "visualize" yourself doing commercials or some kind of on-camera work. You are at least considering the possibility. Very few people just fall into some kind of on-camera career, and visualizing is an important step in accepting your own success.

Nothing you do to help yourself imagine your place in this business is silly. You can cut your picture out and tape it to your TV screen or put it in place of a model's face in a magazine ad. You can give yourself a daily mantra to repeat. But *wishing* you were doing something is not the same thing as *visualizing* you are doing it. Visualizing is a form of acceptance. It is a literal process that uses your imagination to put you in a given situation:

> I can see myself on television, in a commercial. I can see myself standing in front of a camera, auditioning for a job. I can see myself on a film set, working on my lines while they set up lights.

Maybe it seems like another form of meditation, but it's more specific. You can *meditate* on "joyfulness." You can *visualize* yourself laughing, riding the roller coaster. You can also visualize how you would say a certain line on a commercial that you have seen, if you were the actor doing it.

Beyond the necessary first step of visualizing yourself in this business, you can use this form of imagining to prepare, specifically, for auditions and jobs. Your mind has to take in a lot of stimuli at an audition or a job, a lot of surprises. You can help prepare yourself by picturing in your mind the room you will be standing in, by picturing the table where the casting people sit. You can picture where the camera is located, and how you will stand or sit. Once you get in the room, it may not be like you imagined, but you will already have a plan for yourself from which you can work. It is easier to modify that plan than to make everything up as you go along, with no preparation for what you expected.

The next step for you to take in visualizing has to do with how you will read the copy once you are in the room. You need to place yourself in some environment appropriate to the copy.

Let's take that cruise ship copy:

IMAGINE THE EXCITEMENT OF VISITING THE SEAPORTS OF SPANISH PIRATES . . . IMAGINE WALKING ON COBBLESTONE STREETS OVER FOUR HUNDRED YEARS OLD . . . IMAGINE LUXURIOUS, DUTY-FREE SHOPPING, AND MILES OF SILKY WHITE-SAND BEACHES . . .

You are in the casting room, in front of the camera. Now, where are you? Let's say you are standing on a dock, on one of the vacation islands you have seen in photos, or have been to. Behind you is an old, double-masted schooner. You look at the ship, and then turn to camera and say, "Imagine the excitement of visiting . . ."

Now, honestly, don't you think your eyes will be more alive with excitement — you will be more convincing — if you have visualized yourself on some island rather than if you just start talking to the camera with no particular image in mind?

Visualizing needs to be part of your preparation for the business in general, and for an audition or a job in particular.

Don't wish for it — see yourself doing it.

Exercising

Show business includes all body types and shapes. You don't need to be able to run a six-minute mile to do commercials or films. But being in show business does mean using your body to express yourself. So, whatever shape you are in, you want to be able to use what you have as well as possible.

The main purpose of exercises, as far as we are concerned, is not to get you on the cover of an exercise magazine. The exercises that we suggest are to "free the instrument," to limber you up, to reduce tension, to improve your enunciation. But if you can run a six-minute mile, you can skip this chapter.

Tension is a part of life in general, and it is a part of show business, in particular. When we get tense, our muscles tighten, our bodies are less expressive, and our speech is less clear. Stretching, in any form, helps reduce tension. If you have some favorite stretches, do them before you go to the audition, or as you wait to go in. When you are on the set and you feel your energy sagging, some stretching exercises will wake you up and reenergize you.

The most obvious place we carry tension is in our necks, so roll your head around, slowly. Then, lift and roll your shoulders, together and separately. Stop doing any stretch or exercise that hurts. Pain is a warning from your body.

From a standing position, relax yourself over at the waist, as though you are going to touch your toes, and then slowly pull yourself up. Imagine a string attached to the base of your neck, pulling you up. Keep your head and neck relaxed, and just let them fall into an upright position.

For loosening your upper body, you can try this. Raise each arm, one at a time, straight up, and reach as high as you can. Keep your feet flat on the floor, spread apart about shoulder-width, for stability. Alternately, raise each arm and stretch upward, nice and slow, about six times each. Then, reach up and over your head and to the other side, as though you are going to grab the ear on the other side of your head. Gently bend your whole upper body in the direction you are reaching.

To awaken and strengthen your abdominal muscles, blow out in short, quick bursts, as though you are trying to blow out a candle that is three feet away. Do that a dozen or so times. If you feel any dizziness, stop so you don't hyperventilate. You can graduate to panting, like a dog. It is a very difficult thing to do, but it's a great abdominal exercise.

To continue relaxing, just let your arms hang down straight, and then shake them, letting your hands flop freely, to reduce tension in your hands. Open and close your hands slowly, stretching them open, and then closing them to a fist.

You can do any of these stretching exercises whether you are dressed in a suit and tie, shorts, or a swimsuit, and just these few are plenty to warm up your "instrument" for a job or an audition. Flexibility and reduced tension are the goals of these or any stretching exercises that you do. You want to feel loose and free. You want your shoulders down and relaxed, not up around your neck.

Including regular exercise in your life will absolutely make you a better performer. It promotes flexibility, reduces tension, improves your breathing and your ability to use oxygen, and will make you more positive and confident. Maybe, exercise will help you live longer and have a better quality of life as well. I'm certain it will help you as a performer.

Finally, when you exercise, and also when you don't exercise, drink plenty of water. People think they drink lots of water, but usually they don't. You should be drinking about eight glasses a day. That's about a gallon, or a glass every two hours. By the time you feel thirsty, you have already begun to dehydrate. Your vocal chords are one of the first places that dehydration will show up. Your voice gets rough, dry, and scratchy. Coffee may soothe you with its warmth, but it works as a diuretic, and therefore dries you out even more. Nothing you do will help more to keep your voice supple and to increase your vocal endurance than drinking enough water.

Cheers!

4

Advanced Techniques

One of the great aspects of this business is that you can continue to learn and improve your abilities at almost any age. You can begin a professional on-camera career as a child (Screen Actors Guild allows membership at age four), or you can begin working on-camera well after you have retired from another profession, as many of our students have. In some ways, it is very easy to get into show business, and because of that, you'll sometimes feel that everyone on the set has more training than you. But all you have to do to get better is to pay attention. Because of the subjective nature of acting, often you will learn the most about your own work by observing others, by watching how they do things, by learning from their mistakes and how they solve their problems.

Your ability to learn from others is limited only by your own willingness. Academy Award–winner Liam Neeson was asked by Harry Smith in a CBS interview if he had learned anything working with Meryl Streep. Mr. Neeson said yes, and explained how he had observed that Ms. Streep always took a length of time after the director said "action" to gather her concentration fully; she never started talking until she was completely ready. With the high cost of film production, Mr. Neeson said he felt a need not to waste any time. She taught him about not hurrying. At every level, you can learn from those around you.

In this chapter, we'll pass along some of the particular lessons we have learned, well into our own careers, from directors and actors with whom we have worked. For all of us in this business, there is no better teacher than experience. Find every opportunity you can to practice your craft, and observe others.

If you are just starting out and not yet getting work as an actor, then volunteer to work as an usher at a local theatre. Try to visit a film set or get a job sweeping the place up. Classes with other actors, taught by working professionals, can be a great help as well. But nothing can replace the experience you will gain from working, from being around the work and the people who do it.

There came a time when, although I had worked extensively on stage and in commercials and corporate films, I wanted a shot at playing a role in a feature film. I thought my acting skills would transfer to movie work, but I had never been on a feature film set. From what I had heard, commercials and industrial films were very low-anxiety events compared to a major movie set.

So I registered with an agency that books "extras" on movies. I booked a few jobs, and when I wasn't actually working (which is most of the time on a film set), I spent as much time as possible standing where I could watch the director and the scenes being filmed. The differences in movie work seemed to do mostly with the scope and size of production, and the different jargon used. Scenes take much longer to film, and to save the principal actors' energy, they employ stand-ins (the B team) during the lengthy lighting process. (This is not something you will have in commercials and corporate films.)

All that I learned on those few "extra" jobs enabled me to feel at ease and confident when I booked my first principal role in a feature film.

In 5-4-3-2-1

Several years ago, I was rehearsing the national tour of *Cabaret*. The director was the legendary Harold Prince, universally admired and respected for his directing and producing skills on Broadway.

I was making an entrance with a young actress, and she was through the door first. Somewhat exasperated, Mr. Prince stopped her, and in a loud and clear voice, said to her something like, "Ms. _____, would you please start acting before you arrive onstage. *Come* from someplace!"

I stood by, sympathetically, grateful that she had blocked his view of me, since I had made the same kind of entrance. I dodged the bullet myself, but I have never forgotten the lesson.

On camera, you will rarely see anyone make an entrance, in the same sense as on stage. Most scenes pick up on life in progress, and the principle in "Come from someplace!" has particular relevance. The audience needs to get a sense of what led up to that moment.

For instance, with *Cabaret*, when we walked onstage, were we coming from a hallway or outside? Had we been talking or not? Were we friends or strangers? Those are the kinds of things that won't be scripted, and yet they are what brings the energy and reality into a scene.

When you audition, and even on some jobs, you won't have the reality of scenery — a set — to help you tell the story. It's up to you to invent the moment before your dialogue begins, before we see you. Mentally, you need to invent the physical surroundings of the scene and what your character might be doing before the scene begins. It doesn't need to be complex. But the more clearly you imagine that moment before you begin "acting," the more real your character will seem.

You are at the audition. They roll tape, you slate your name, and then you begin. Someone may or may not say "action." Take plenty of time to begin. Those seconds between your slate and your dialogue, or between "action" and your dialogue, are when you come to life as a character. Don't feel rushed! It's your time. Use it to imagine where your character is, and what he or she is doing when the dialogue begins. In that way, you will be "coming from someplace" when your scene begins.

Let's say you are auditioning for a doctor in a commercial. Your first line is, "PEOPLE ASK ME ALL THE TIME WHAT PAIN MEDICINE I TAKE." You might decide to imagine that you are looking up from reading a medical chart just before you begin your line. You could use the script for your prop chart. Maybe you have a ballpoint pen that you use to make a mark on the "chart," and as you are putting away your pen, you look up and begin your line. These are natural things that a doctor does, and will give a sense of reality to your reading. Of course, you can do the same without using any props. Just clearly imagine a circumstance that is logical for the lines you are given.

The actual job will be different. Most likely, the director and/or the set on which you are working will provide you with the physical circumstances. You can work within that reality to invent what you might be doing as you begin your scene. However, even on the job, you may still have to imagine everything. More and more, directors are shooting in front of a "blue-screen," or "Chromakey," which is a solid background of one color, and not always blue. Then, in the editing process, a computer will replace that background with whatever scenery or action they want. They can use stock footage, or still photos, or they can shoot you and the background separately, and assemble them in editing. (If this process is used, then you cannot wear anything "blue," because the computer will paint the background onto that color anywhere it sees it.)

In addition, on the job, much more will happen before you get to begin acting, and you will have to maintain your own focus. In general, after you are dressed and made up and on the set where you need to be, it will go one of a couple ways. If they are recording both picture and sound on a videotape camera, then the director will trigger the camera and give you some kind of "action" cue, much like at an audition. Invariably, someone will be adjusting lights or something and you will have to wait for your cue.

If a film camera is being used, the director will call, "Roll camera," and the camera operator (sometimes called the DP or Director of Photography) plus the person operating the separate sound recorder will say, "Speed," after the machines have reached full speed and are properly operating. There might then be some additional "tweaking" of the lights before the director finally says "action." (Some say things like "Go," or "Anytime.")

You bring your character to life wherever you can in that sequence, and begin the scene when you are ready after the director's cue. Again, don't feel rushed, and whether you are ready to begin or not, allow a small space after the "action" cue before you begin speaking, so there is room for a clean edit.

Within this sequence, you may need patience and total concentration. On a recent shoot of mine, after we had gotten a couple of good takes, the director decided to redirect the scene. He rolled camera, and I began concentrating on the new direction. We got "speed," but then because of a bad reflection, the DP started fussing with one of the lights. When that didn't work, he began moving the prop I was holding, to get rid of the reflection. He seemed happy, but an assistant bumped the leg of the camera, and the DP had to refocus. Then the sound man asked us to hold for an airplane that was going over. My arm was starting to cramp from the odd angle of the prop, and the makeup artist came over to powder a shine on my forehead. The camera was still rolling, and I was fighting to remember the redirection of the scene. Finally, a full three or four minutes after I was set and they had rolled camera, the director called "action."

In those situations, you have to *keep breathing* and focus completely on your character and whatever reality you are playing. Try to ignore everything else. Just staying relaxed is a chore, but you have to do that and also focus on the scene, and how it begins.

The famous "In 5-4-3-2-1" takes the place of the "action" cue on daytime dramas, situation comedies, and other multicamera television shows that have to be timed to fit schedules, but you won't actually hear the "2-1." The stage manager will count those manually on his or her fingers under the lens of the camera that is coming on first. The last two numbers are silent to allow for a little flexibility for what exact point the show goes "on the air."

If, by the way, you ever do work on a daytime drama, it is during the countdown that you will need to start whatever action you have — not the dialogue — but whatever action leads into your scene. The implication of the countdown is that "go" comes after the 5-4-3-2-1, but again, the director may later choose to pick up the scene a bit earlier. You need to be doing something, or you risk a scolding from the stage manager (I speak from experience).

The circumstances will vary with the type of show you are doing, and the style of the director, but the need for you to "begin acting" prior to where the script begins is consistent. With commercials and films, whether on the audition or the job, you will not have any countdown to worry about, and you don't need to feel rushed. But decide where your character is "coming from," physically and mentally, just before the scripted scene begins, and you will begin your scene alive and energized.

Specificity

I was fortunate to be in the original Broadway cast of Stephen Sondheim's musical *Passion*, written and directed by James Lapine. Mr. Lapine had won a Pulitzer Prize, so I thought I could probably learn a thing or two from him. Here is my favorite of the many things I learned.

We were having a note session after one of our preview performances. Two women played nurses in the show, and he asked one of them what she had been doing in a particular scene. She responded, "I don't know, I'm just playing a generic nurse." He was not happy. He told

61

her, "Don't be generic, *ever*, in life or in my show." Great advice, on both counts.

Being a generic nurse made no statement whatsoever. It wasn't interesting. Your character may be a nurse or a cowboy, but that is not playable. You play a *person* who happens to be a nurse or cowboy. What is interesting to watch is how the nurse/cowboy feels or thinks or acts in the given situation. How did the nurse feel about the woman she was caring for? Did she want to be there, or somewhere else? What did she think of the young soldier nearby? There are lots of possibilities, all quite specific. Later, when the actress spent the scene attending the sick woman but all the while subtly "checking out" the soldier, it made the scene and her character quite interesting to watch.

Everything you can learn about acting in general will apply to working in front of the camera. However, because of the intimate nature of the camera, because you are seen from so close up, honesty and simplicity are all important. You have to boil the acting down to its most pure form. You must be completely specific.

Of course, ideally, the concept of specificity should apply to all forms of acting, but the camera will always catch you if you are not specific — if you are dishonest or unfocused.

The concept of specificity is very simple, yet it's the first thing to go out the window when we get nervous or distracted. But specific choices will anchor you and make the essential inner dialogue feel natural.

The catch is you will almost always have to make the choices on your own. The casting person at the audition, or even the director on the set, will say "Have fun with it" or "Just give me a nice warm and friendly read." Those are not specific, and you can't *play* those. You have to make choices that *result* in "having fun" or "being warm."

If a casting person or director says to "have fun," the result they are looking for is perhaps like a situation comedy on TV. The lines are quickly paced without thoughtful pauses, the characters are slightly exaggerated, and there is a feeling of fun like when you and a gang of your friends are telling jokes to one another. Your way of achieving that result is to pick up the cues and to choose a thought or attitude that puts a twinkle in your eyes or a laugh in your voice.

Let's say it's a corporate film script of a casual meeting. In real life those meetings often begin with some jovial comments before they get down to business. You could add a laugh, as though a joke was just told. You could lean toward another actor, real or imagined, and in a quiet voice, improvise a line like "He said that?" or "I think so too!" Say it with a little laugh, and then begin your scripted line, "WELL, AT TODAY'S MEETING . . ." In that way, you help create an undercurrent of humor, or a good-natured rapport between your character and the others at the meeting.

Our nurse in *Passion* was an Italian character in a dramatic piece set in the early 1800s. As an actor in a corporate film or commercial, you will most often be playing yourself. Of course, it could be a corporate film in which you demonstrate the proper use of some piece of medical equipment, and you might still be portraying a nurse. But whether you playing a nurse in a modern-day corporate film or a nurse in a nineteenth-century period musical, your goal as an actor should be the same: to provide a specific undercurrent of thought and/or attitude that makes the character believable and interesting.

The technique of providing yourself with real, unspoken, inner dialogue will work to make an improvised scene with no spoken lines more believable, and it will work to make a dialogue scene with other characters more interesting and real.

If, however, you are delivering a monologue to camera, in the category of commercials known as "spokesman," the inner dialogue doesn't work in the same way. Here, you need to choose a specific attitude or thought with which to deliver your lines.

In her book and teachings, Joan See speaks of these as "verbal actions," and she includes as examples confiding, confessing, challenging, asking a question, letting the cat out of the bag, defending yourself, sharing, admitting (see Appendix C). The possibilities are endless. Inner thoughts such as these motivate and hold together the ideas you express in your monologue. They add the human quality, the vulnerability, the humor, or whatever you might think is appropriate.

In choosing an inner attitude to motivate your "speech," be aware of its connotation. "I want to share a secret with you . . ." is positive and will connect you to your audience. "I have a lesson to teach you . . ." will distance you from your audience. If you choose to motivate yourself with "apologizing" or "admitting," the connotation includes guilt, which could be useful in adding humor and might also endear you to the audience.

The words on the page might seem negative: "I CAN'T GET MY KIDS TO EAT BREAKFAST . . ." If you choose "sharing a secret," the words now seem positive, and your thoughts will stay connected all the way into where you tell the audience about the great new cereal.

Specificity also applies to actions as well as thoughts. If the script calls for you to pick up a pencil, or straighten your tie, or tie your shoe, or hand over the report, then the only way you can honestly do those things is to honestly do those things. Don't indicate actions. Really do them.

Really doing an action motivates you and provides the same kind of reality that inner dialogue and thoughts do. In addition, performing a specific task causes you to focus on the activity. That concentration has a way of making you very honest, because you're not acting.

As an exercise, try this. Get something to eat — an apple or something other than gum. Now, take a monologue or piece of copy from this book or from any play, and deliver it while you eat the apple or whatever you have to eat. Try it over dinner if you wish. You will find that the words come out very honestly, because you are concentrating on the activity of eating and all of the inner thoughts that go along with eating.

This won't be an appropriate activity for most copy, but the exercise will show you the value of "really doing." This lesson was brought home to me when I was playing a cop on *As the World Turns*. I didn't know how to "be a cop." However, in the scene, I was holding a piece of pie. So, I ate the pie as I delivered my lines. I did know how to do that. The "cop" ended up being very natural. The prop, or more correctly, the activity involving the prop, kept me honest, because I was honestly involved in the activity.

Less Is More

The problem of the "size" of your performance on-camera manifests itself in a couple of different ways, depending on your background. Actors with theatrical backgrounds, used to playing to the back of the house, have trouble making their performance smaller and more contained. Inexperienced performers, unsure of what acting is all about, have trouble keeping themselves natural, and tend to make exaggerated "faces."

The problem is made worse by some directors and casting people, because they are result-oriented. Their concerns are with the final product, whereas we need to worry about the process of getting there. On an industrial shoot for one company, the director asked me to "do that thing with your eyebrows that you did on the audition tape." Fortunately, I was able to replicate the inner dialogue I had used on the audition and create an expression similar to what he remembered (one eyebrow did raise itself in an expression of suspicion).

Confined to the little box of a TV screen, stage actors feel that they *can't* use their arms. Amateurs feel that they *must* use their face. "Eyebrow acting" is the end result in both cases.

Go back to the "Cheer" reaction shot exercise to illustrate your own dependence on your eyebrows. Turn on your camera, or look in a mirror. Bring a piece of cloth up next to your face, look at it, and give to the camera/mirror your own version of a very negative expression. Now bring the cloth up beside your face, look at it, and as you bring your eyes to camera/mirror, say to yourself these actual words: "This is *terrible!*" Let your face do whatever comes naturally when you say those actual words to yourself.

My suspicion is that the first time you knitted your eyebrows, or wrinkled your nose, or shook your head. The second time, when your face expressed what you said, it was far more believable. You still might have raised your eyebrows or something, but probably it looked more real this time.

The size of your performance is determined by two things: the honest expression of a thought or feeling, and how far away from your "audience" you *appear* to be. The camera represents the audience, but it might be in a close-up shot, where you *appear* to be about twelve to eighteen inches away from your audience. You have to deliver the line or expression as though you are talking to someone twelve to eighteen inches away. Practice with a friend, or a camera, or a lamp, one foot away. Use the line from above, or put something sweet in your mouth and say, "This is *good!*"

Now do the same thing to a friend or camera that is about seven feet away, which is how you would appear in a "medium shot." You need only to make your expression big enough to reach across the seven feet.

Finally, try it in a "long shot." Place your friend or the camera thirty or forty feet away. Say the same line in a size appropriate to reach across the thirty or forty feet.

Express yourself honestly and appropriately for how far away you appear to be in the camera, and the size of your performance will be correct. Even if you consider yourself to be a "clown," the comedic expressions you make to someone who is one foot away will be very different from the faces you make to someone seven or eight feet away.

Thanks to modern microphones, hidden in your clothing or hung from a "boom" above your head (often, both), any sounds you utter, no matter how subtle, will be heard. So you don't have to project your voice to be heard. You should use your body *and* your voice in a way that is appropriate to cover the distance that you appear to be away from your audience. Don't let yourself feel "confined" in any way other than that.

The best illustration we have to demonstrate how little you need to "do" to express yourself on camera is to use the extreme close-up (ECU). You can do this with your camera at home, and it will teach you a lot about your ability to express feelings and the camera's ability to record them.

Set the camera up in an ECU of your face, where only your eyes show. Give yourself a few specific thoughts to express. For instance, imagine tasting something sweet and think to yourself, "This is *good!*" Or think about specific things that give you pleasure, irritation, excitement, or confusion. Look down with your eyes between the thoughts you express, and come back up to the lens with the new thought. When you review the tape, you will have no trouble "getting" the thought— knowing what feelings you were having. If you honestly felt or thought something, your eyes will have revealed it.

In feature films, these extreme close-up shots are usually reserved for moments of high drama or affection. You won't have many ECUs in commercials and corporate films. But if you get the concept of what it takes to express yourself in an ECU, then you are on your way to good on-camera acting.

Visualization

One aspect of success in working before a camera is an ability to visualize yourself doing the work, in a "positive thinking" sense. Visualization, in a more literal sense, calls for you to create whole physical surroundings in your mind. On stage, or on a soap opera, or in a feature film shot on location, you might be surrounded with a wonderful and completely authentic physical setting. But on a studio set for a film or commercial, and certainly at the audition, you'll get little help in creating the visual manifestations of time, place, and character. The rational adult in you will be aware of standing on an "X" in front of a camera, with a bunch of people looking on. But your job is to imagine and see where you are in the story you are telling so that the audience can see it too. The more specific you are, the more successful you will be.

In a recent audition for a commercial, Brenna was asked to play a teacher. To help create that visual idea at the audition, and to motivate her first line, she began by turning away from the camera to "write on a blackboard." She then put down her imaginary chalk and dusted off her hands as she turned toward camera to deliver her first line to her imaginary children. She got the job, and on the set that's exactly how the spot began. The director told her that she was the only actor to have done that in the audition, and that it inspired him to shoot the spot that way with her. Her visualization was so specific and strong that it brought to life her entire character.

On the set, she had real chalk and a real blackboard, but just outside of what the camera could see, there was nothing but light stands and stagehands. She still had to visualize the schoolroom and the children.

Recently, I played a reporter covering the aftermath of a hurricane for a disaster preparedness film, and my set was a blue wall. They did try to set up a fan to create a little wind, but it made too much noise, so they had to get rid of it. I was shown some photos of what would be edited onto the background later, and we discussed where I should "picture" each of the things that I was to point out in the report.

Of course, much attention has been given to various feature films in recent years that offer scenes between people and aliens, or people and dinosaurs, or people and natural disasters, all of which were actually shot in front of huge blue or green Chromakey walls, with the various actors fighting only what they could conjure up in their own imaginations.

You clearly see the importance of good visualization skills. All we are asking you to do is to remaster the ability that probably came so easily to you when you were age five. I can't really tell you how to use your imagination, but I *can* tell you how effective you can be when you allow youself to freely imagine, to picture scenes in your "mind's eye," to talk to people who aren't there, to visualize other actors who are there as the characters they portray, to talk to the camera as if it were a friend.

Action

At most auditions, you will be taped or filmed in a medium shot, from the waist up, or perhaps from your head down to your knees. If the scene is a two-person or group scene, the camera will pull back enough to get everyone in, but the grouping will be fairly tight. So you will be limited in the amount of physical action that you can do.

Any action the casting agent or director asks you to do will be an approximation of what they expect the finished commercial or film to be. The most complex action I can recall being asked to perform at an audition is to pretend that I was getting into a car. (We'll include that in the list of MOS exercises in Appendix B.)

Usually, your action will be limited to small things like handing someone a report, tasting something, picking up a product, or simply walking into frame. If the copy you receive is printed in the left-right format, with copy on the right and video directions on the left, then the left side may indicate some action that you could approximate. Whatever you do in the form of action, keep it simple and real so that it enhances your performance and does not distract you or distract the people watching you.

Actions that you are given, or that you choose for yourself, can have undesirable consequences. In a recent class, the actor working on copy from a political spot on a "soft drink tax" chose to start with a soft drink can in her hand, and then punctuate the spot by tossing the can over her shoulder at the end. Very interesting idea! However, when we watched the replay, the action with the can was distracting. It helped catch our attention at first, but after she gestured with the can in the opening and then continued just holding the can as she spoke, I found myself watching the can to see what she was going to do with it. I missed the message of what she was saying altogether. She would have done better to put the can down, after the opening, and then pick it up again for the "button." There was nothing for her to do with the can during the main part of the copy, it looked out of place in her hand, and she was uncomfortable holding it, so it drew our attention.

Let reality and common sense be your guide when you choose an action. If the action you choose seems unnatural or feels without purpose, it will probably look that way on tape as well.

Pacing

Pacing, as a concept, is complex and very subjective. It is not defined by how fast you are speaking. In fact, slowing down may make the reading of a line more interesting, increase the audience's interest, and therefore make the pace *seem* faster.

The key to *good* pacing is variety—variety in your speed, in your pitch, and in the emphasis you place on words and phrases. Variety of pacing not only helps hold the audience's interest, it also focuses their attention on the ideas that you wish to emphasize.

So you might begin your reading of a piece of copy with a quick, energetic pace, but then slow down when you come to a key phrase or an idea you want to emphasize, such as a product name or the main benefit of that product. You "billboard" the key idea in a passage with your change of pace. It is a technique that will come naturally to you after a while, and you want to use it sparingly. Slow down too many phrases and none stand out. But try to choose the one or two ideas within a piece of copy that deserve special emphasis, and mark them. Then consciously slow down and it will focus the listeners' attention.

Look at this piece, for example:

I'M CHEWING GUM AGAIN. IT'S WONDERFUL! FOR YEARS I COULDN'T BECAUSE GUM STUCK TO MY DENTAL WORK.

BUT NOW THERE'S *DENTIFREE GUM*. IT DOESN'T STICK. SO I CAN ENJOY ALL THE PLEASURES OF CHEWING GUM AGAIN. THE DELICIOUS FLAVOR, FRESH CLEAN BREATH, AND REFRESHING TASTE . . . ALL THAT'S POSSIBLE AGAIN WITH *DENTIFREE*. TRY IT IN PEPPERMINT AND NEW SPEARMINT. DENTIFREE GUM . . . YOU'LL LOVE IT.

In this piece, the most important idea to get across is "IT DOESN'T STICK," and I would slow that phrase down for emphasis. Next in importance would be "THE DELICIOUS FLAVOR, FRESH CLEAN BREATH, AND REFRESHING TASTE." This also needs some vocal "underlining."

Probably the best way you can affect the pace in a conversation between two or more people is to shorten, or lengthen, the time between lines. When you want the pace to be fast, you "pick up the cues," or you allow little or no time between one actor's lines and another's. Taking more time between lines will have the effect of making the scene seem much slower, even if it really isn't.

If a director or casting person tells you to "take the air out," they mean to take out any pauses. By itself, that doesn't mean to speed up your rate of speech; it just means to pick the cues up faster.

A "situation comedy" type of commercial would call for a faster pace and allow little or no space between the lines. A more serious "business" conversation in a corporate film might include actual pauses. Good pacing will match the piece.

The qualities you can use to affect the pace of a piece to keep it interesting are endless. You can speed up and raise the pitch of your voice to add excitement. But you can also add excitement by slowing down and intensifying your voice, like with a stage whisper.

Here again, observation can be a great teacher. Listen to conversations around you at work, or when you are waiting in line at the movies or at the food court in the mall. Listen to the variety in people's voices as they relate stories to one another.

As a part of good acting, you must pace your scenes in a way that holds people's interest. Plan the pacing as a part of your rehearsal, and be aware of it as you perform.

TelePrompTers

Most people are familiar with the concept of a TelePrompTer. It is a piece of equipment that is attached directly over the camera lens, or is placed in the speaker's eyeline, with the text of what is to be said reflected onto an angled piece of glass so the person speaking can read the script and still appear to be looking into the lens or out at the audience. The two applications that you most frequently see are with television newspeople and with public speakers, such as the president. (You've probably noticed those two angled glass screens to each side of his podium.)

TelePrompTers are almost never used for commercials. The copy is fairly short and can be memorized ahead of time or while the actor is getting into makeup and the crew is lighting the set. The exception to this is with very long commercial copy, such as infomercials, or when the spokesperson is a celebrity or nonactor who doesn't memorize well.

For industrial films, especially for any type of narration, TelePrompTers are frequently used. They allow the writers to make changes up to the moment of shooting, and they allow the actors to deliver scripts that are often technical and difficult to remember without a mistake. TelePrompTers save time and money for the producer, and they save mental stress for the actor.

Once in a great while, you will have a TelePrompTer for an audition, usually in the case of a government agency or a corporation that has an in-house film department with a staff prompter operator. But it is rare for most auditions, because hiring the equipment and an operator runs about $500 a day, and there is no need for that expenditure at an audition.

The techniques for using a TelePrompTer well are not difficult. The trick is not to look like you are reading. Some practice will help you to become proficient, but there are some things to concentrate on *not* doing. Don't scan your eyes back and forth like you do with the page of a book, don't lock your eyes on one spot on the screen, and don't squint in concentration. Think of it as letting the words come to you, with your eyes focused generally in the central area of the lens or screen, without staring or fixing your eyes on one spot.

The TelePrompTer operator will adjust the speed of the passing words to match your pace, slowing down and speeding up when you do. If the operator is moving too fast or too slow, it is important for you to say so. They should follow your pace, not the other way around. It is important that you don't feel like you are trying to keep up with the TelePrompTer. That will happen sometimes. As long as you are keeping up, the operator won't know that the speed is too fast. So if you feel the machine is rushing you, ask them to slow it down a bit. Overall, you will find that most operators are very good at following your pace. That's their job.

"Hard news" and more serious narration requires a style of full eye contact with the lens. But if you have any kind of narration or dialogue that allows you to break your focus and look away from the lens for an instant, doing so will help you appear as though you are not reading. Of course, that requires you to know the script well enough to remember a few words in advance. The trick is not to search for your place when you return to the screen. However, a little rehearsal, and trusting that the words will still be there when you return your eyes to the screen, will allow you to do this with confidence.

One of the best places to use this technique of looking away for a moment is with a "walk and talk" (which is just what it sounds like), because of the casualness implied by your walking. When you look away it has the appearance that you are coming up with the words, or looking for inspiration.

When you do a job on a TelePrompTer, you will often be provided a "hard copy" of the preliminary script in advance of the shoot, although with the heavy dependence on computers now, some writers type the script onto a disk and send it right into the TelePrompTer. But if you get a copy of the script, read it through enough to become familiar with the language and to find any problem spots, such as difficult-to-pronounce phrases, acronyms, or trade names.

When you arrive on set, say hello, and pick up any last-minute script changes. Then introduce yourself to the TelePrompTer operator and ask to rehearse with just the two of you, so that you can get used to one another, and so that he or she can adjust to your rhythms and tempos.

Think of the TelePrompTer operator as your best friend on the set. Treat that person well, and your day can be a whole lot easier. Also, if you are ever offered a TelePrompTer, even when you know the script (which has happened to me), accept the offer. With the confusion and the delays and the nervousness on a set, it is wonderful to have a crutch for your memory.

Again, don't lock your eyes on the words, trust your peripheral vision, and, if you are having any trouble seeing the screen because of a light in your eyes or a bad reflection, speak up. You are the only one who can see the screen, and the only one who knows if there is a problem.

Earprompters

Simply put, an "earprompter" is an audio system that provides a prerecorded script directly into one of your ears, and cues you word for word. It consists of a speaker that fits into the ear, which attaches by hard wire or audio transmitter to a sound source, usually a miniature cassette recorder. There are many variations on the equipment, all the way up to switches that attach to your big toes for starting and stopping the tape player.

The earprompter concept is sort of an audio version of the Tele-PrompTer. The studio, however, won't have one. If you have an interest or a need, then you put together a system of your own, or purchase one that is ready-made. For some applications, such as a location shot where a TelePrompTer is not a possibility, having the ability to work with an earprompter will allow you to deliver pages of dialogue without memorizing.

I use mine extensively for live narrations at trade shows and for industrial films where TelePrompTers are not possible. For instance, I recently did a shot where I had to deliver quite a bit of dialogue while driving down a highway. The camera was mounted on the hood (so a TelePrompTer was not a possibility), and I had to concentrate on not crashing the car. Using an earprompter allowed me to deliver letter-perfect dialogue (that had just been written) and still concentrate on driving.

When we did get back to the studio, they wanted to shoot mostly hand-held camera shots for the "conference" scenes. Again, no Tele-PrompTer was possible. I was handed new script pages, I recorded them on my earprompter, and we shot the scene.

Using an earprompter is not difficult. However, it does take considerable practice and concentration before it feels comfortable and natural. You can test the idea by recording any script or material on a tape recorder. Then play it back and repeat the words as you hear them. You speak about two or three words behind what you are hearing. It seems intimidating at first, but once you get the hang of it, you'll love it.

To practice "developing an ear" for this type of work, we suggest practicing by talking two or three words behind whoever is on your local radio talk show. If you think you will have an interest in learning this technique, then practice it frequently, and it will soon become just a matter of concentration.

If, by the way, a producer or an agent asks you if you can work with an earprompter, for your own sake, please do not say you can until you really can. I watched one actor try to learn on the job. As the camera rolled, her eyes fixed into a stare of concentration, sweat poured down her face, and she took more than twenty takes to get the first couple of lines. The day went into overtime, and she will never work for that production company again. I suspect that her agent will be reluctant to call her again, as well.

But having the ability to use an "ear" can help get you jobs in some markets. I still don't see them used much in New York City, but in Chicago, Washington, D.C., Atlanta, and many other large markets, the ability to work with an "ear" is a requirement on more and more jobs.

If you do want to invest in an earprompter system, buy good equipment. It won't help you to become skilled at doing this only to have equipment that works against you.

You have probably noticed the curly silicone tube that runs down the neck of newscasters. The tube attaches to a hollow mold that fits into the ear. At the other end, the tube attaches to the earpiece speaker behind your back or hidden in your clothing. The earpiece speaker then attaches to a miniature recorder, or whatever sound source you desire. In the case of newscasters, they are getting information from producers or directors, as well as getting cues and listening to conversations of interviews. This type of system is a "hardwire" system, and will not cost you much.

For a "hardwire" system, you can go to a commercial electronics outlet that has them or you can order announcer's equipment from a professional sound supplier. Call a local TV newsroom and ask their engineer where he or she buys from. Telex is probably the brand they use. The principal component you need is a Telex RTR 04 Telethin speaker, with a Telex CMT 92 (or similar) cord. You can get the silicone earpiece and tube that attaches to the Telex speaker from a hearing aid supplier like Audiophone.

A "wireless" system consists of a tiny "hearing aid" type of instrument that goes into your ear, and an electronic loop that goes around your neck, which transmits the sound to the earpiece. The loop around your neck attaches to the sound source by way of whatever switches you desire. This system can be somewhat expensive and has to be custom-made by one of the companies that specialize in these systems. Wireless systems start at about $300 to $500 for just the basics. Then you can add on from there.

The systems are an investment in dollars and time, but if you book one good narration job that requires an earprompter, then you are ahead already. A great many executives are also using earprompters to deliver speeches that seem extemporaneous. So you might put it to use in more than one area of your life if you have multiple occupations.

To purchase "remote" or "wireless" systems, you can contact these companies:

Sargon Yonon Hearing Aid Center
67 E. Madison, Suite 1415
Chicago, IL 60603
(312) 872-7007

Cardinal Sound (generic system)
2317 Kansas Avenue
Silver Spring, MD 20910
(301) 589-3700
www.cardinalproaudio.com

Ear-Talk Inc.
PO Box 17
Bates City, MO 64011
(800) 828-1990

Instant Memory Performer's Technologies
PO Box 52541
Atlanta, GA 30355
(404) 233-0283

This supplier also offers excellent training:

Brian Collins—Earprompter Speaker Training
527 Acacia Avenue
Solana Beach, CA 92075
(888) 327-7766
www.earprompter.com

Once you have a system to practice with, record the speech you wish to deliver in a clear and steady voice. Overenunciate the words on the tape and don't put in too much inflection. You can soften and add emphasis in your delivery, but you have to be able to hear plainly all of the words. If you make any little mistakes on your recording, rerecord it. Otherwise, you will include those in your speech. You will say exactly what you hear.

When you practice with an earprompter system, deliver your lines to a mirror. Novice users get that "deer caught in the headlights" stare and lock their body in concentration. It is unavoidable. That's why you don't want to try to fake it. Practice with your system in front of a mirror or on a video camera until you are able to look around with your eyes, move your body freely, and gesture with your hands. Then add in a distraction or two, like some music playing or someone walking around you, and you will have an idea of a working situation. As soon as you feel comfortable and capable of concentrating on your words and delivering them with the proper feeling and inflection, then you are ready to add this new skill to your résumé.

Hand Work

Very few people outside our business are aware that "hand work" is a whole separate category in on-camera work. Although for years my wife has worked as a "hand model," shooting what is referred to as "tabletop" in commercials, the hand work that we will spend the most time discussing here is the work that you will be asked to do as a part of your work in industrial films. Rarely will you be asked to do any kind of "product shot" in commercials. In fact, the close-up shot of someone handling the product in a commercial is usually done by the hand model, who is an expert at handling the product for the camera. He or she will be able to hit imaginary marks in midair time after time, will hold the product absolutely still and at the proper angle for the lighting, will pour or slice the product perfectly, and will also have beautiful hands (small and beautiful for food and regular products, long and beautiful for lipstick and jewelry).

Let's say a sponsor wants to hire a celebrity spokesperson for their product. The celebrity films the "spokes" part, and then goes home. Then the hand model comes in to film all of the close-up shots with the product that will be inserted into the commercial. When we watch the spot, we think that it is the celebrity lifting up that bottle of whatever. In fact, although many celebrities are very attractive people, they might not have great hands, and they certainly aren't trained hand models. So a hand model handles the product shots.

The stories that I think are most interesting along this line are when a hand model is used for the hands of an actor or celebrity while that celebrity is actually doing the spokes part. The celebrity is talking, and the hand model is down on the floor, or under the table, or squeezed in behind the celebrity, and is holding up and demonstrating the product so that in the camera the hands appear to be connected to the person talking. When you open a magazine and look at some print ad, the hands touching that lovely person's face might not be hers or his. In fact, there are "parts models" who specialize in portraying all sorts of body parts for ads: feet, ears, ankles, legs, etc. The unions for actors in commercials have negotiated the minimum scale payments for this kind of work, roughly the same as for the actor. The only difference is that residual or "use" payments are not made to the hand model. But the hand model also doesn't have any conflict. The hand model can work for Coca-Cola today and Pepsi tomorrow. The actor can't do that.

Of course, many commercials consist of product shots only, with no spokesperson. One of the jobs of the hand model is to make you notice the product and not the hands, but the next time you watch commercials, take notice of how many times you can see hands doing something in a spot. You will be surprised.

Hand work in industrial films is considerably less critical or specific, and the actors in those films are usually asked to do their own hand shots, usually something like typing on a computer, handling a report, or something along those lines. As a part of your audition for both industrials and commercials, you will sometimes be asked to show your hands when you do your slate. Unless you are asked to do otherwise, always show them with the fingers extending upward and the fingers straight but relaxed. Show them near (but not blocking) your face, showing first one side of the hands and then the other. The reason you don't show them pointing downward is that the veins on the backs of your hands fill up with blood in that position, and they look bulging and less attractive.

Pay attention to your hands. Unless you want to learn hand modeling specifically, you don't need to worry about perfection. But you do need to go to auditions with clean hands and well-groomed nails. If you were painting the house last night, take the time to get the paint off your hands. It may sound silly or picky, but clients scrutinize you. You are going to be representing them and their companies, and they won't take the time to understand if you didn't get a chance to clean up your hands. If a woman has been wearing black or neon orange nail polish, she should change to something more neutral for an audition or a job. None of us need the added stress of having to show our hands on camera when we know they are not in good shape.

5

Preparation (Is Everything)

One of the great ironies to me about this business is the seemingly "last minute" aspect to everything having to do with choosing actors for commercials and films. It is very common for you to get a call on Tuesday afternoon to go to a Wednesday audition for something that shoots on Thursday. The client works for weeks or even months to prepare a project, planning, budgeting, scripting, etc. Then, when it is time to choose the individual who will actually carry the message to the viewer, to choose the actor who will bring the project to life, the client waits until the last minute. It seems to say they aren't too worried about getting the right actor and having that actor be available.

Well, the fact is that choosing the actor is simply the last step in the process, and there probably will be a very good selection of actors who are available. So, if you are going to be a part of that process, your preparation has to begin well before you get that call for the audition. Working successfully in commercials and film requires the actor to always be ready for that "last minute" call.

Luck is a word often associated with our business. But, the right preparation—combined with the right look—will get you jobs in this business. You can save luck for the lottery.

The most fundamental ingredients in your preparation are a good headshot, a basic wardrobe, ability, and confidence. Of course, it doesn't stop there, but in this section we will help you with the basics. Even if you already have a headshot, the section on photography will help you with your next photo session, and it will be valuable for evaluating what you have now.

Things happen very quickly in this business. We want you to be prepared and to hit them with your best shot.

Headshots

Whether you've been doing this for twenty years, you are just about to finish school, or are just starting a second career, everyone shares the same need for a good headshot.

Before you get a talent agent to represent you, before you see the casting agent and get an audition, before you set up an appointment with an independent film director, your first "meeting" with those people is usually between them and your photo and résumé. It is your headshot that usually makes the first impression. With that in mind, you should consider the well-known expression, "You don't get a second chance to make a first impression."

Your headshot is your calling card—the way that you introduce yourself to nearly everyone that you come in contact with professionally. It is a mobile job interview. It has to be of good quality, it has to look like you, and you have to be happy with it.

In short, a good headshot will open up more opportunities for you in this business than anything else, and a bad one will do just as much to hold you back.

Even though you need the photo "yesterday," don't rush into getting it. You want your headshot to represent the absolute best "you," and that takes some preparation. If the headshot you now have doesn't look like you, or you feel embarrassed by its quality, throw it away and start over. It is only hurting your chances for success.

Your first consideration in preparing for a good headshot is to know what you are "selling." Actors like to believe that they could play anything, but the reality is that they can't, if only because producers and directors will hire someone who "looks the part." Your photo needs to represent you and your "look" as people in the industry will see you.

For instance, we had a student who had been a physician for twenty years, but on-camera he looked more like a blue-collar worker. He would make the perfect "cabbie." Until he saw himself in replays, he didn't know how to market himself. On stage, you can stretch the limits, but with camera acting you must, to a large degree, stay within— and even embrace—your own stereotype. It's not who you would *like* to be, it is who you *seem* to be.

We had another fellow who was a wonderful character actor, with good comic instincts. He showed us a photo of himself, posing with a pistol. He wanted to be on "cop" shows. But, he doesn't *look* like a cop, or a criminal. He looks like the friendly neighbor, or the guy sitting on his cabin porch, selling you oatmeal. His headshot should not argue with that reality.

I always wanted to play the "bad guy." But I look wholesome, "all-American." I have a good smile and *dimples*, for crying out loud. So, at least on camera, I have to play (and, in fact, I *get* to play) myself, a fairly regular, middle-American "dad."

You may not be sure of how you appear to others. Look in magazine print ads in mainstream magazines like *Newsweek* and *Good House-keeping*. Unless you are a fashion model, stay away from modeling magazines. Watch TV ads. What are the people who look like you playing? You *are* there, because advertisers use *all* types, especially the "real people" types.

Then you have to consider how you can enhance your look. If you look like a "mom," notice how the "moms" are wearing their hair. If you look like a college student, how are they dressing in the ads? Some things that you may love—like having a beard, or that radical new hairstyle, or that *old* hairstyle that you just don't want to change—will limit your ability to look the part.

You have to make choices here. The things that might make you look great when you go dancing Friday night, like that new ring through your eyebrow, will severely limit your chances at success on-camera. There is an irony here as well. Success in acting on-camera requires, among other things, for you to be natural and to play yourself, but you also have to fit into an image. So, as much fun as it would be to shave your head, you have to know how completely that would limit your work in commercials and film. You have to establish your look for your headshot, and then you have to maintain it, at least generally. Again, it serves little purpose to spend the money it takes to get a good headshot and then radically alter your look. Producers and directors need to know how you look now. If they see your headshot, think you are right for something, and then call you in only to find out that you don't look like that at all, it wastes their time, and that ends up hurting you.

Finally, if there is something that makes you feel self-conscious or less expressive and makeup won't cover it up, like a chipped tooth or a mole where you don't like it, get it fixed before you shoot your new shot. Good photos are all about what we see in your eyes, but, just like for the motion camera, if something physical is inhibiting your ability to express yourself comfortably, fix it.

Getting a new headshot can be a bit of a pain. But, the good thing is that you usually only need one good shot. Once you have it, you can reproduce it, get it into circulation, and let it start working for you. Yes, they sometimes end up in the trash, but they also end up in people's files, and provide you with opportunities long after you forgot even sending it out.

Choose carefully who you get to reproduce the shot. Again, the cheapest is almost never the best. For children's headshots, which have to be replaced every six months or so, we think you can scrimp a little on quality of reproduction. But, for adult actors whose headshots will be out there representing them for years, the quality of the reproduction service should match the quality of your photograph.

Also, be sure to have the reprint service print your name on the photo. We do not recommend printing your résumé directly on the back of the photo. Résumés will be updated far more often than the headshot, so print your résumé separately and attach it to the back of the reproduction. Make sure your résumé has a contact number, but don't put your address. Headshots sometimes end up in strange places; they don't need your address.

Photographers

Once you have a good idea of what you want your photo to say about you, how you fit into the marketplace, and how you appear on-camera, it's time to find a photographer. Talk to other actors; word of mouth is one of the best ways to find someone good. Unfortunately, if you are not in New York City, Los Angeles, or some other major show business city, you may have only a few choices, because even the finest photographer may not be good at headshots, and you don't want a "portrait" of yourself.

Once you find someone promising, ask to meet them and look at their work. A good rapport between you and the photographer is the most important ingredient for a successful shoot. If, when you meet them, you find that your personalities clash, you should think twice about using them, no matter how good they might be with someone else.

You know that good photographs cost money. However, because of the importance of a good headshot, this is not the place for you to shop for price. Now, if you have two photographers that you love, and one charges $600 and the other charges $300, then you might let price make your choice for you. But, in general, you will get what you pay for, and you don't want "cheap" to be the impression others get when they look at your shot.

There are books such as *The Actor's Picture/Résumé Book* (see Appendix C) that will help you plan for a headshot. Here are a few questions and thoughts that you might keep in mind when you shop for your photographer. It's your money, so be prepared and get what you want.

1. Exactly what is included in the shooting fee? (How many rolls of film will we shoot, etc.)
2. How many prints are included?
3. Who owns the negatives?
4. How many changes of wardrobe or hairstyles are included?
5. Do you have a makeup artist, and is that a separate fee?
6. How long is the session, and will I be the only one shot at that scheduled time?
7. How soon can I see the contact sheets?
8. What kind of guarantee do you offer, and is there a charge if a reshoot is needed?
9. How much are extra prints?
10. How far in advance do I need to book, and do you require a deposit or cancellation fee?

Any photographer you choose will give you an idea of what to bring and how to prepare for your shoot. But, if you haven't done a *commercial* headshot before, or you are not familiar with black-and-white photography in general, you will find valuable information in the "Pre-Session Information" (reprinted in Appendix D).

Makeup and Hairstyles

Makeup

The degree to which you will be responsible for your own makeup (or wardrobe) varies with the market and the medium.

Women For headshots, if you are female, your makeup should be done by a professional makeup stylist who is familiar with black-and-white photography. (Color headshots are good for print work and modeling, but are absolutely unnecessary for commercial, theatre, or corporate shots.) If you are going to go to the trouble to get a good photographer and then good reprints, there is no point in sabotaging the finished product with poor makeup. The makeup you wear in everyday life, no matter how well it is applied, is most likely not appropriate for photography. Your headshot will be looked at next to other actors' headshots, and those actors will have used professional makeup. You want your headshot to stand up with the best. In addition, your headshot represents your potential appearance for a job, where you will have professional makeup.

Even if you have a beautiful "natural" complexion, makeup is a reality. It is a tool for enhancing your role, whether you want to tone down for a "blue collar" or "outdoors" type, or you want to add sophistication for an "upscale" type.

The caution is to make sure that your makeup does not compete against the "type" you are presenting. You don't want glamorous makeup unless you are shooting a "soap" shot, and the makeup for "casual mom" is different from that of "business woman." Again, for your headshot, your best bet is to work with a makeup stylist.

For auditions, you will be doing your own makeup. You want to enhance the idea of the character you will be playing, so don't just automatically put on what you normally wear. A "waitress" in a commercial might seem to have on very little makeup or way too much, depending on how you want to approach the character. When you get the call for the audition, find out what they know about the character so you can make some choices in how you want to appear.

Men Men, perhaps unfairly, can probably get by with very little makeup for their headshots. Again, this is in keeping with what will happen on the job. Clients usually want the men not to look "made-up." Men's makeup is corrective—to cover blemishes or to even skin tones and get rid of any shine on the skin. You should avoid any shiny appearance to the skin unless you are supposed to look like you are sweating. A flat base or powder will probably do the job, and you should keep that on hand. If your eyebrows are very pale, you might brush a bit of color into them, just to make them stand out a little. Just avoid *looking* like you are wearing makeup.

In fact, I think that men should avoid makeup altogether for auditions unless you need to cover up some blemish that appeared overnight, or you want to *very subtly* matte down a shine with some translucent powder. Unless you are good at applying it, it can really make you stand out, and not in a good way.

Makeup Artists and Makeup Kits When you are booked for a commercial, you will most likely have a professional makeup person, whether the job is "union" or not. Makeup artists do not generally have union affiliation, and they are not restricted to working one way or another. For an industrial/corporate film, whether or not you have a makeup stylist will depend on the market and the budget of the project, rather than on whether or not the talent is "union." I have had to do my own makeup for Xerox; another time I had the best artist in town for a local grocery chain. Always ask if makeup will be provided on a job, and keep a basic makeup kit ready for those times when it is not. For men, some matte foundation or powder, an eyebrow pencil, and maybe some lip gloss is about all you will need. For women, your usual makeup kit will probably do fine. You don't need the heavy "theatrical" makeup generally used on stage. Camera shots are intimate, and subtlety is the key.

Hairstyles
When you go to a job where makeup will be provided, it is generally best to arrive with your hair mostly ready, and either little or no makeup on. Makeup people might touch up your hair a little if it needs it, but they are not hairstylists. Unless you are told that a hairstylist will also be provided, it is not good form to show up in rollers.

As for your hair, at auditions follow the same guidelines as you do for makeup, trying to do what would be appropriate for the character. Just keep in mind that your face needs to show. Long bangs or a style that allows the hair to fall down and cover much of your face does not benefit you, regardless of how "stylish" it might be. The guidelines are the same for men and women. A male actor, auditioning for a "business executive," shouldn't show up with shaggy hair. Executives are well-groomed people, so make sure to clean up your neck.

These may seem like small details that have nothing to do with acting. But they have everything to do with how you look, and if you don't look right, you probably won't be seriously considered for the job.

Wardrobe

I have heard many stories from casting people about how someone "got the job" when they walked in the door. Often, it was simply an attitude they possessed. Just as often, it had to do with the fact that the wardrobe they chose, and the way in which they presented themselves, perfectly suggested the character for which they were auditioning.

One director told me about a time when he was auditioning actors for the role of a fisherman. One actor came in with a fishing vest and a hat with several fishing lures attached. With just those two pieces, the actor had already achieved the most important task in getting cast in the commercial: he looked the part. The director told me that he remembered hoping that the fellow could act, because he was sure that he would be the art director's choice. The art director had the final say. It turned out that his acting was fine, even if, on the job, they had to show the actor which end of the fishing pole to hold. He didn't have a clue. But it didn't matter because he looked the part all the way, thanks to the borrowed bits of wardrobe.

Chapter 6 has several other anecdotes on the subject of how wardrobe can play a part in casting. Of course, the fisherman example is quite specific. Often, the description of the character is just something like "dad," or "business person," or "IBM employee." But, for most characters, you can find some "uniform" aspect to their appearance, and you are smart if you make sure the wardrobe works in favor of the character. I don't think you should go overboard, and you don't need to spend a lot of money. But a small investment in some wardrobe items that are basic to the characters for which you might audition can pay off handsomely.

Certainly, if you are a good bet for playing a business person, then you should have a business suit, a dress shirt (blue or off-white, for men), and appropriate shoes. Not everyone agrees with me on this, but I don't think you can successfully play a business person wearing a suit jacket, jeans, and sneakers, even if you are only being shot from the waist up. I see a lot of people go to auditions that way, because they want to be more comfortable. However, part of the aspect of the uniform is how it affects your posture and carriage.

A pair of work boots, jeans or khaki pants, and a long-sleeved plaid shirt suggests "blue collar" or "construction" for men or women. But, it is the boots that do the most to make the statement. Wear the same outfit with slip-on penny loafers or sneakers and you could be a "casual dad." If you are getting called for a doctor or medical worker, you might consider spending a few dollars for a used lab coat. Again, it is just a suggestion of the character that you want to make. You don't need a tool belt packed with drills for a construction worker, or a briefcase full of forms and calculators to play an accountant. Too much wardrobe or paraphernalia can just get in your way, or expose the fact that you aren't really comfortable wearing it. But, by all means, let everything about your appearance suggest the character for which you are auditioning.

When you book the job, what you need to provide in terms of wardrobe will again depend on the market and the budget for the project. Other actors can tell you what usually happens in your area. In some cities, like New York, producers like to provide everything in order to maintain complete control, and the card you fill out at the audition will ask you for your sizes. In other cities, producers provide almost nothing, preferring instead to pay you "rental" for your clothes. (Screen Actor's Guild contracts provide that you be paid $15 for each outfit used.) For industrial and print work, because "business" types predominate, you will probably need to have a small selection of business suits (two or three).

Whatever audition and work clothing you have, keep them in good shape and ready to wear. It is a last-minute business, and having clothes that are ready to go helps your work go smoothly and lessens your anxiety. You don't want to tear through your closet the morning of a big audition only to find your good suit or blouse wadded up on the floor waiting to go to the cleaners.

Many actors like to think that they can play anything wearing black pants and a black top, and perhaps they are right if it is Shakespeare. But with commercials and corporate films, and perhaps even musicals and feature films, the more that you can do to look the part when you walk in the door, the more successful you will be.

Sample Reels

Everyone in our business needs a headshot. People who are interested in doing print work (modeling, still photography) need a "comp card," a composite of shots from print work that you have already done, or shots you have taken that show you in potential modeling situations (business look, bathing suit, formal wear, casual mom, etc.).

Actors involved in commercials and industrial films (especially on-camera narrations) are sometimes very well served by having a sample "demo reel." Sample reels, or demo tapes, are like a video comp card, a collection of pieces from work that you have done, assembled onto a two- to four-minute video cassette that you can distribute, upon request, to potential clients. For actors who do voice work, an audio-cassette—again, around three minutes long—with radio spots, narrations, or other voiceover pieces serves the same purpose of auditioning for you, without your having to be there.

Occasionally, instead of holding a regular casting session, producers find it convenient and/or cost effective to call an agency and ask for submissions of demo tapes from which they can cast a project. Or, they might just select talent from the library of tapes they have on file. Auditions are time-consuming and expensive for producers, and some would rather see examples of your work in projects similar to theirs. Once in a while, a producer will hold a regular audition and then ask to see the reels of those in whom he or she is most interested.

Audio reels can be synthesized in a studio. An actor can record various bits of copy and then have the engineer add music and sound effects to make it sound like the real thing. There are companies that will help you put together an audio reel. Look for them in one of the theatrical trade magazines, or ask other actors. Word of mouth is usually the most reliable source.

"Faking" a video reel is not really possible because of the cost in-volved. So, whenever possible, get a copy of any work that you do. Most producers will send you a copy once they have finished the film and made copies for distribution. *Always* offer to pay for the copy. Most likely, they will send you a VHS copy for free. If you want or need a three-quarter-inch copy, they might ask you to pay their cost or provide them with a blank tape, because "three-quarter" is very expensive. It does offer higher quality duplication and you have less "second genera-tion" loss. However, these days, most studios can electronically en-hance VHS to provide very good copies. We have stopped asking for anything but VHS, mostly because the less complicated you make it for the producer, the more likely you will actually get a copy.

Once you have a few pieces of work, you can take them to a local video editor for assembly into a "master reel," which *should* be three-quarter-inch. From your master, you can have VHS copies run off at that studio or at a duplication service. Expect to pay around $5 to $6 per copy, which may include a computer-printed label. You can be as creative as you wish for the box, which will cost you accordingly. Make sure that your name is on the spine of the box. We also choose to have a photo on the cover of the box.

Demo reels should not be much longer than three minutes. A pro-ducer probably won't watch or listen to more than that. You want a fast-paced selection of short pieces. If you have a narration, you might include one longer section of that to show how you handle a long piece.

Because it is mostly industrial producers that hire from demo tapes, you are better off to put mostly industrial work on these reels. Industrial films have a very different energy from commercials. If you are short of material and have a copy of a commercial that you have done, you can include it for variety.

Audio reels are usually separated into "commercial" and "narration" reels — either separate reels altogether or divided on the A and B sides of the same tape.

Before you spend money on any of this, however, talk to people in your area to see if tapes are a useful way to market yourself. In all hon-esty, in the last ten years of working in New York City, between the two of us we have been asked for a demo reel only *one* time. However, in other markets, such as Washington, D.C., and Chicago, many actors book one-third or more of their work directly from their demo reels. In those markets, the expense and effort of putting together and maintaining a sample reel is more than justified.

6

In Their Own Words
Wisdom from Agents, Producers, and Directors

In the process of conceiving this book, we realized how valuable it would be to have input from the people who are working, right now, in the casting process. So, we sent a list of three questions to a mixture of about twenty professional casting directors, talent agents, producers, and directors, each busy and highly respected in their own field.

We had hoped to have the insight of at least a few of them. We were overwhelmed when nearly every person responded. It confirmed our belief that the people "on the other side of the table" want you to be good, and they were willing to share their feelings of how to help you accomplish that.

These are the people that you actually audition for, the people who hire you. Each of them has their own point of reference to the process; a couple of the directors who contributed also direct on Broadway. The comments of each reflect concerns that are specific to their part of the process, and yet you will find many common themes.

If you only read part of this book, read this chapter. It would cost you hundreds of dollars to attend seminars in New York to hear these same people say these things. I plan to read their words again myself, regularly.

We decided to publish them word for word, expletives and all. The passion with which they responded is as instructive as their opinions, and we didn't want to edit a thing. Our final contributor gave us several pages of anecdotes that will instruct, and probably entertain, you. At least it did us.

Practice the lessons of this chapter, and you will work in this business. For those of you already working, the instruction in these pages offers you the opportunity to greatly increase the rate at which you book jobs.

Stuart Howard
Casting Director, New York

At an audition or interview, what gets your attention in a positive way?

Strong choices from an actor who is prepared.

What is a common thing actors do to "blow" an audition?

Assume that the casting director wants them to fail—viewing the casting director as an enemy. This is crap! I have never, ever met a casting director who does not want the actor to be superb: After all, selfishly, we get the credit for finding the talent.

My job is made easier by actors who . . .

Understand that this is a *business*. It still amazes me how many actors are unprepared and thoroughly unprofessional.

Ken Slevin
Artist's Representative, New York

At an audition or interview, what gets your attention in a positive way?

A warm, open, positive attitude. An actor who has a strong sense of self, but yet isn't antagonistic, and is willing to work hand in hand with their agent to be very successful.

What is a common thing actors do to "blow" an audition?

Play it safe.

My job is made easier by actors who . . .

Show up to auditions on time, have a current 8 x 10 that is a true representation of themselves, and book their expected ratio of jobs.

Jack O'Brien
Director for Broadway
Artistic Director, Old Globe Theatre

At an audition or interview, what gets your attention in a positive way?

I'm most impressed by thoroughly professionally behaving people who walk in, prepossessed, pleasant, but not pushy—*not* trying to perform as they enter the room—decently and respectfully dressed, prepared, who attack the work at hand with relish and diligence, but aren't above giving a spark of wit and interest to the table as well. And briskly out the door.

What is a common thing actors do to "blow" an audition?

I think the major error in auditioning is trying to please the auditioner as opposed to oneself. When I know the person I am auditioning is both easy with the material and genuinely seems to like it, I'm all attention, even if it isn't what I thought I wanted. Trying too hard, seeking to find what the table wants, is the ultimate sin. Please *yourself*. Even if you don't get the job, you become instantly memorable.

My job is made easier by actors who . . .

Are not needy. Actors who come in with a positive attitude and aren't trying to find a justification for either their life or their lack of position will always continue to work with me. I find the word *play* interesting. We're putting on a *play*. Surely that has something to do with the best attack on work. I'm here to enjoy myself as well as accomplish something.

Benita Hofstetter
Casting Director, Washington, D.C.

At an audition or interview, what gets your attention in a positive way?

Showing up on time, being prepared, professionally dressed. Know as much as you can about what you are auditioning for . . . not asking a lot of questions, just trusting that who you are is MORE THAN LIKELY what the producer is looking for . . . not telling your life story before or after the audition, NEVER making excuses, and never judging your own audition.

What is a common thing actors do to "blow" an audition?

Not being prepared by not understanding what the character should be like and not knowing the copy well enough to make sense of the text. Also, actors OFTEN are rude to the check-in person or assistant or drill that person with questions about who else is cast, and personal questions about the casting director, producer, director. Just because someone is young or not in the audition room, they may have ENORMOUS influence and will tell the casting director if they think an actor is going to be problematic on the set.

My job is made easier by actors who . . .

Return phone calls promptly, don't tell me the story of their day or life, don't talk endlessly why they are sorry but they can't be available . . . let me know when they move out of town, or when their number or union status changes . . . call to cancel an audition if not able to attend . . . come prepared with copy and correct "look," arrive ON TIME or earlier, and remain professional with EVERYONE they come in contact with once booked on the job.

Lucille Slattery
Artist's Representative, New York

At an audition or interview, what gets your attention in a positive way?

First impressions are always important. Neatly styled hair and makeup, comfortable but conservative dress. Good teeth and a professional approach, i.e., organized, prompt, and friendly. A great headshot. Direct eye contact to camera and a beautiful smile. Minimal touch-ups.

What is a common thing actors do to "blow" an audition?

#1—*Say too much* to casting directors. My feeling has always been — go in, get the job done, and get out. Any problems or questions should be called into the agent or manager after the audition. Nosing around or trying to do something other than what's directed is a definite turnoff.

My job is made easier by actors who . . .

Act and leave their egos at home! And act professionally in all business situations.

Marcia Mitchell
Producer, Washington, D.C.

At an audition or interview, what gets your attention in a positive way?

94

A certain presence—an "I can do it" attitude, intelligence, and—always—humor. If someone displays humor, that tells me they're confident. I think people who are good are also nice.

What is a common thing actors do to "blow" an audition?

Whine or fuss over direction. Talk about personal problems. Suck up.

My job is made easier by actors who . . .

Understand the job at hand; bring something to it of their own; be generous with the other actors and contribute to a "team" approach.

Mike Lemon
Casting Director, Philadelphia

At an audition or interview, what gets your attention in a positive way?

Someone who is prepared, focused, and pleasant, who takes risks and makes strong interesting choices, who is flexible and follows directions, who is excited about the process and being alive!

What is a common thing actors do to "blow" an audition?

It's critical that actors use their waiting time wisely preparing the audition material, that they make strong, interesting choices, that they listen and respond to any direction given, that they exude a quiet confidence and save any bravado for their performance; that they are engaging and personable, that they bring headshots and résumés, show up early, and wait patiently.

My job is made easier by actors who . . .

Listen, focus, read instructions, prepare their materials, ask good questions, smile, and enjoy the process.

David Bell
Director-Playwright, New York

At an audition or interview, what gets your attention in a positive way?

An audition starts from the moment the actor enters the room. Everything he/she does is observed and offers clues about the auditioner. The experienced actor will be very professional and prepared, and yet will project a sense of self anyway.

What is a common thing actors do to "blow" an audition?

They don't listen. The most common problem with auditions generally involve instruction or adjustments given to actors, who are too nervous to listen. Often, the actor who has waited thirty minutes in the waiting room working on the given script— enters the audition, having figured out *exactly* how to deliver the material— sometimes to the exclusion of the words of advice given by the director or casting director. If I really liked an auditioner, I will attempt to "chat" with them after their piece— in order to get a sense of the person. I am often surprised by the number of actors who simply ignore the question, because they were not expecting it—or get defensive and suspicious of anyone who speaks to them.

My job is made easier by actors who . . .

Understand the process of actor selection. Professionals always understand that a million disparate criteria are being addressed by the casting director— are you too old? too tall? do you look right for the role?— are obviously questions being asked—*but also*— a good director will ask himself if his image of the role might be altered to accommodate a good actor. An actor must never "second guess" the process— and understand that it *is* a process.

Scott Rosenman
Producer, Baltimore

At an audition or interview, what gets your attention in a positive way?

Display passion, emotion, and a willingness to put inhibitions aside.

What is a common thing actors do to "blow" an audition?

Fail to focus on the task at hand.

My job is made easier by actors who . . .

Allow themselves to enjoy their assignments.

Jackie Kelly
Casting Director, New York

At an audition or interview, what gets your attention in a positive way?

A good first reading.

What is a common thing actors do to "blow" an audition?

Read poorly.

My job is made easier by actors who . . .

Arrive at a casting session on time . . . know why they are there . . . what part they're reading for . . . and are dressed accordingly.

Fred Hanson
Director for Broadway, New York

At an audition or interview, what gets your attention in a positive way?

A natural and personal connection to the material, and of course, talent!

What is a common thing actors do to "blow" an audition?

Select inappropriate material to audition with, or come unprepared.

My job is made easier by actors who . . .

Make specific choices, even if I think they're the wrong ones! It's better to see someone's take on the material than to see a bland audition.

Ellie Vitt
Producer, Washington, D.C.

At an audition or interview, what gets your attention in a positive way?

1. Dressing for the role. 2. Positive attitude and willingness to hang around so we can audition them with others.

What is a common thing actors do to "blow" an audition?

1 = Attitude.

My job is made easier by actors who . . .

1. Learn their lines!!! 2. Bring wardrobe variety (and clean)! 3. Don't complain!

Pat Moran, CSA
Casting Director, Baltimore

At an audition or interview, what gets your attention in a positive way?

Firstly, the theatre experience on the résumé gets our attention. Secondly, the more conversational the audition is (as opposed to acting with your eyebrows) the better. Acting is all about believing the actor is the character.

What is a common thing actors do to "blow" an audition?

Showing up late is certainly not a plus. However, since our method of auditioning is the "cold read," we *always* preface with instructions to "stay on the book!!" Many actors refuse to listen and blow the audition by trying to commit a passage to memory in ten minutes—I can see them grasping for the words and suffering their performance—I can assure you not an actor alive has ever gotten a job from being able to memorize on a cold read. We have never said, "Let's hire her, she sure can memorize."

My job is made easier by actors who . . .

Show up on time—and do not chat it up with others in the waiting room while another actor is auditioning. Also, by following any instructions we may give.

Steve Fairchild
Director, New York

At an audition or interview, what gets your attention in a positive way?

A friendly, but not overfriendly, demeanor and a professional attitude is the first thing that attracts me. Also, does the person look right for the part? Of course, there may be little an actor can do because I'm coming to the meeting with a certain need in my mind. But, a good reading might change my mind or at least open it to new possibilities. Confidence is important too. A confident professional will ask me good questions and try to determine what I want.

What is a common thing actors do to "blow" an audition?

If an actor seems to need too much "care and feeding," it could very well overshadow their positives.

My job is made easier by actors who . . .

Are on time and ready to work. Frankly, an actor is a part of a team that includes craftpeople, writers, and artists. . . . Experience, professionalism, talent, and confidence all make a difference, in no particular order.

Kathy Wickline
Casting Director, Philadelphia

At an audition or interview, what gets your attention in a positive way?

Feeling confident and enthusiastic about the product or service that they are auditioning for, and asking questions on the character, to the director. This shows genuine interest on the part of the actor and opens up a dialogue that leads to a creative audition.

What is a common thing actors do to "blow" an audition?

Being unprepared, no pic and résumé, running late or entering unfocused . . . Apologizing for "messing up" on the script, not listening to direction.

My job is made easier by actors who . . .

Come with all details in regard to audition time, and shoot date availability is a *must*. We never want to see an actor who is unavailable for the shoot date. Ironically, some actors do not understand this.

Sonny Coyne
Casting Director-Producer, New York

At an audition or interview, what gets your attention in a positive way?

When an actor arrives on time for his interview, quietly signs in — and peruses script, he makes points.

What is a common thing actors do to "blow" an audition?

Actors who come in acting almost too important to be here at all. Very cocky, smart-alecky actors are a complete turnoff to me. We enjoy actors who are respectful, polite, and understand we are here to do a good job and get the most and best from them.

My job is made easier by actors who . . .

Come here eager and pleasant, dressed according to specs given them by their agent. Recently, casting for Burger King— a young man came here sporting a Burger King cap— he almost got the job, but it still goes to the most talented.

Our last contributor misplaced her questionnaire, but had plenty to say, which she entitled, "Stream-of-Consciousness Thoughts About Auditions."

Kay Lorraine
Producer, Honolulu, Hawaii

Things that I have actually seen actors do in auditions that I just couldn't *believe*:

- Come into an audition smelling like last night's beer bust.
- Stop the audition to tell a dirty joke.
- Ask the client personal questions.
- Show up an hour late without calling.
- Badmouth another actor in front of the client.
- Make fun of the client's product.
- Bring their girlfriend or boyfriend to the audition and ask if it's OK if he/she sits in on the audition.
- Assure the producer that they know how to ride a horse or bicycle, or swim or whatever, when they really can't. Also, please don't tell us that you just love animals or kids if you're scared to death of dogs and have no interest in children.

Perfectly normal stuff that often occurs:

In every audition, I will see several actors who are so nervous that they don't/can't listen to the instructions. Instead, they bob their heads up and down wildly saying, uh huh, uh huh or OK, OK, OK after every third word they hear. And you know darn well that they aren't really *hearing* any of it. They are just so desperate to appear knowledgeable and agreeable that if you told them you were going to mutilate their private parts, they would just nod in agreement and say, "Right!"

Actors are often afraid to ask questions for fear of appearing dumb. Nobody expects you to know everything the minute you walk in the door. It's OK to ask questions. But try real hard not to ask "What's my motivation?" It's so cliché. Instead ask "Am I angry? Am I confused?"

Things that piss us off:

Don't write "Commercial Credits Available Upon Request" on your résumé. Yes, I know that misguided agents advise talent to do this, based on the idea that you're protecting yourself by keeping the client in the dark. Here's the deal, folks: This is the audition and this *is* the request. No games. I automatically assume that when there are no commercial credits on the résumé, that the words "Commercial Credits Available Upon Request" are just a deception to hide the fact that the actor has no experience and no credits. It lowers you in my eyes.

Don't come to the audition without knowing that you are free to do the job. Don't tell me about your current McDonald's spot *after* the client has already fallen in love with you in the Burger King audition. Don't mention the 7:00 P.M. curtain or dinner-hour waitress job *after* you've been booked for an 8:30 A.M. call time. Don't assume that this shoot will be over in eight hours, unless you have an agreement with the producer to that effect *prior* to the booking. This is, unfortunately, not a nine-to-five job.

Don't use your audition time to promote other projects that you have going on. Don't interrupt the audition process to ask me if I saw your television guest spot last Thursday night. Don't try to get me to commit to coming to your new play. Don't suggest that I remove the audition tape from the tape machine so that we can all look at your updated reel. Don't pass out flyers promoting your upcoming concert or your improvisational comedy troupe. Just concentrate on the *audition you're in.*

Don't "forget" to pay your AFTRA/SAG dues even though you promised to take care of it the day before the shoot. Unfortunately, the unions use us producers to enforce *their* problems with *their* members. If you fail to sign in (or out) at the audition, guess who the union yells at? The actor? Guess again. They yell at whoever is running the audition. Before I can hire you, I have to get clearance with the union office. If you are behind in your dues, I can't shoot. And if you promise to handle it and come to the shoot without having done so, they fine *me*. Not the actor. Not the actor's agent. They fine the production company. This will not endear you to me. And I promise to tell everybody in town about it, too.

Unless it is specifically a sexy part, don't show up at the audition in a micro mini and a tank top. I'll get confused about just what business you are in. And don't come on to my director, either. You have no idea what my relationship is to him; or to his wife.

Don't engage my client in chatty conversation. Not at the audition. Not at the shoot. Without ever meaning to do so, in your attempt to be friendly and memorable, you can sometimes cause no end of problems. Let me give you an example: During the course of a shoot a few years back, an actor with a minor role engaged the out-of-town client in small talk. In his eagerness to find some common ground in the conversation, the actor mentioned the name of his friend and brought the entire shoot to a dead stop. What the actor didn't know was that his friend had just taken a new job with an advertising agency that had recently begun working for the client's primary competitor. The client and his competitor were in a fierce battle for market share. And the campaign on which the actor was working was the client's big "secret weapon" in that battle. That's *why* they were shooting out of town. Filming was halted while the client went through several hours of grueling long-distance calls, consulting on whether to scrap the shoot or just get rid of the actor. In the end, the actor was sent home; but not before signing a hastily drawn confidentiality agreement. Was the client unreasonably paranoid? Absolutely. Clients are often unreasonably paranoid. You never know what will set them off. Answer questions pleasantly, smile, and volunteer nothing.

Between the time of the booking and the actual shoot date, please do not cut or change your hair color, shave your mustache, or otherwise alter the way you looked at the time of your audition, without first discussing it with the producer or the director. Like it or not, a large part of what you have to sell is your "look." Remember that old Holiday Inn slogan: *The best surprise is no surprise*.

If I could give actors only one piece of advice or insight in this business, it would be this: *Stop beating yourself up, emotionally*. The truth is that nothing, absolutely *nothing* you could have done would have gotten you the job. *You just weren't what they had in mind*.

A million years ago, when I was trying to break into the business as an actress (and believe me, no one ever accused me of being a "talent"), my very best performance in each audition took place about five minutes after and three blocks away from the audition. I always peaked in the parking lot. Do you know what I mean? You run the copy over and over in your head as you are leaving the studio, replaying every second that you were in the room. And just before the garage attendant brings down your car, *you figure it out!* The perfect interpretation. The exact right attitude. You are overwhelmed with the urge to run back to the audition and *beg* them to let you read it again so that they can send home all the other actors that are waiting in the lobby and *hire you on the spot*.

Ever wish you could be a little mouse in the corner and find out what really happens when the actors all leave the room? Well, I moved to the other side of the camera. I eventually became a producer. For the last eighteen years, *I have been that little mouse in the corner*. Now I am going to tell you the truth about what goes on in that room: When you walked through the door and they saw you, the overwhelming odds are that *right then and there, you didn't get the part*. You were too tall. You were too short. You were too old. You were too young. You were too "ethnic." You weren't ethnic enough. You looked too preppie. You looked too sexy. You looked too much like the girl next door. You didn't look enough like the girl next door. You looked too ordinary. You looked too different. They didn't like your hair. They didn't like your eyebrows. They suspected that they wouldn't have liked your *mother's* eyebrows. *You just weren't what they had in mind*.

No amount of natural performing talent would have made you taller. There aren't enough acting classes in the would to make you shorter. And the best nose job in the world will only make you look a bit less "ethnic." Stop beating yourself up. Four times out of five, nothing you could have done or said would have made the least bit of difference.

Let me give you some examples of what I am talking about (absolutely true stories, every one).

Story #1 It was a national hot dog spot. The storyboard was drawn showing a woman with straight-cut brown hair, about two inches above the shoulder, wearing oversized, kind-of-squarish glasses. It wasn't a drawing of anyone in particular. It's just what the art director thought of when he envisioned the mom of a ten-year-old in his mind's eye. We auditioned about thirty actresses. At least a dozen of them would have been excellent in the role. Guess who got the job? A lady in her thirties who had brown hair, cut straight about two inches above her shoulders. And in the audition, she happened to wear oversized glasses that had a square cut to them. How could she *fail* to get the job? Not only was she a fine actress with a good feel for the dialogue, she was *just exactly what the art director had in mind!*

Story #2 The script required a perky, wholesome spokeswoman. At a group preproduction luncheon just before going into the auditions, we were all talking about what kind of person we should be looking for in the part. At one point the client remarked that his ideal would be an enthusiastic twenty-year-old volleyball player or a bubbly college cheerleader. In the course of the afternoon auditions, we saw lots of perky, trim, physically fit, attractive young ladies. About one-third of the group could interpret the copy well and had the right look and attitude. Then, during a lull in the action, the client began perusing the résumés. One of the women we were auditioning was a college student. Her résumé listed her extracurricular activities, including French club, cheerleading squad, and volleyball team. Guess who got the job? *She was everything the client had in mind.*

Story #3 At the conclusion of auditions for a McDonald's commercial, it was clear to the director that the little redheaded twelve-year-old boy was perfect for the spot. Everyone in the room agreed, except the advertising agency producer, who would not even *consider* the boy. After much arguing, the forty-year-old Jewish agency producer held his ground and revealed his reason. "When I was a kid, there were three redheaded brothers who used to chase me home from school everyday, yelling 'kike' and brandishing big sticks. I still have nightmares about those redheaded kids." And that was the end of the discussion. The role was given to a different boy.

Story #4 We needed to cast a husband-and-wife couple for a United Airlines spot. We found a wonderful woman who had just the right touch of warmth and sparkle. She was 5'10". We had lots of men over 6' to choose from. Unfortunately, none of them was exactly what we had in mind. You know the story—too stiff, too nerdy, too old, too young, too preppy-looking, too handsome for words, etc. Our favorite male by far was a terrific actor who happened to be 5'9". The client was not comfortable casting a couple in which the wife was taller than the husband. Unfair? Sure. But in the end, the part of the wife was awarded not to the best actress, but to the best actress under 5'7". What performance could that fine actress have pulled off to act *smaller*? Nothing.

Story #5 Another McDonald's commercial. One young actor arrived at callbacks only to discover that he was the only one called back for that role. He thought he had the rent covered for that month. Wrong. During the final casting, the favorite counter girl turned out to be a beautiful seventeen-year-old African American actress. Unfortunately, her natural black dialect couldn't quite wrap itself around the client's name. It came out *MacDownald's* every single time, even after dialect coaching. We can overlook many things; mispronouncing the name of the advertiser, however, is not one of them. The next favorite counter girl was Caucasian. Casting her in the role would eliminate any minority representation in the spot. Nobody felt comfortable with that decision. So we hauled out the videotape from the original audition session and found an excellent African American performer who could play the customer just as well as the guy we had planned to use. The original actor never knew what hit him.

Story #6 We needed a family for a water heater national dealer promo. The client absolutely insisted on casting one particular actress in the part of the bitchy, nagging wife. Frankly, she was a nice lady, but a dreadful actress who cost us an extra hour during the shoot just getting out one line correctly. Still, the client insisted on proceeding with her. "She looks exactly like my ex-wife," he explained. "What a shrew. I hate her. *She's exactly what I had in mind when I wrote this spot!*"

The moral of these stories: Casting is one of the most subjective decisions in the world. Flipping a coin would be more scientific. Probably, four times out of five, you already didn't get the part when you walked in the door. Other than making certain that you look clean and normal (that would eliminate multicolored hair, black nail polish, or four holes in each ear), there's nothing much that you can do about the way you look. What you *can* do something about is the other 20 percent: how you handle yourself, how you interpret copy, your ability to follow direction, the tricks of the trade, understanding the protocol, doing the work that it took to get you to the audition in the first place. All of that you can control.

Go in there and give it your best shot. Then move on to the next audition.

7

The Job

Because of the importance of auditions, their difficulty and their necessity, we focus most of this book and most of the classes that we teach on the audition process. However, as teachers, we do not serve you if we don't prepare you for the job itself, at least in a general sense.

Certainly, every job is different, and you learn the ropes very quickly once you start working on-camera. But, a film or commercial set can be a place of high anxiety, especially if you arrive not knowing what to expect and what is expected of you. The mood on a set is often very good natured, with a spirit of great fun. That is especially true if the crew has worked together a lot. Underneath the fun, however, there is usually a sense of pressure and tension, because the future success of a product or a program is often dependent on the results of that day's work. If the client is on the set, the pressure multiplies. For the ad agency or the executive in charge of the project, the result of that day might affect the future of their jobs.

For that reason, you have to do everything you can to be prepared, to concentrate, and to stay calm. Don't be fooled by the joviality, or thrown off if things seem tense. In either case, the mood usually has nothing to do with you.

This is not a business where showing up on time and working hard will get you a promotion. But, jobs do lead to other jobs, and professionalism— combined with some talent—will be remembered.

When you book a job, as you are getting the details of call times, wardrobe, script, and so on, be sure to get a phone number for the studio or shoot location. If something happens to delay you— a late subway train, or a crash on the beltway—you can call to say you are on the way.

When you get to the studio or location, find a production assistant or an assistant director (PA or AD) and check in. They'll guide you to makeup and wardrobe, or at least to a holding area. You will then begin what seems like a long day of waiting. Once they are ready for you, they are invariably ready *right now*. So, once you are made-up and dressed, it is up to you to stay ready and not wander off just because no one has spoken to you for two hours. Just take a book.

The days are long, so pace yourself. You need to be able to deliver the same performance energy after three hours of waiting as you would have at the beginning of the day.

When you are on the set, observe everyone; they will be your best teachers. But, concentrate on what *your* job is. There is always much distraction. You have to tune out the random conversation, and the sound man pulling at your clothes to adjust your microphone, and the time of day, and anything else that wants to distract you.

If they do ten takes of your scene, or five, or twenty, the majority of them won't be usable because of some errant technical problem. That's when you have to remind yourself to concentrate and to stay calm. You will eventually get a good take, or two, with all of the elements working, and it is up to you to seem as fresh and energetic on take 12 as on take 2.

Keep in mind also that everyone on the set is watching what involves *them*, lights, sound, camera dolly, and so on, and they may declare as "unusable" what you felt was your best take. Don't let it frustrate you; just give another good one. Also, as friendly and fun as film sets can really be, there usually aren't a lot of congratulations and backslapping when the day is done. *Your* work may be finished, but *they* have days of editing and postproduction to do.

Props and Continuity

Props add a level of opportunity and responsibility for an actor. Using a prop tends to keep you honest and natural in your acting, because habit and "muscle memory" take over when you use a familiar thing. You don't have to "act" to use a pen, or open a book, or tie your shoe. If you tried to pantomime doing any of these things, it probably wouldn't look right, at least not in the intimate view of a camera. So, being able to really use a prop is great for playing a scene. It motivates you physically and gives you natural motion. It also helps to lessen your preoccupation with the words themselves.

In return, you have a responsibility for the "continuity" of the props that you use. On some big commercial shoots, there will be a person in charge of continuity. They will constantly be taking Polaroid photos of you and the set in order to remember later where the props were from take to take and scene to scene. However, on most sets, even if someone is taking Polaroids from time to time, you will need to keep track of your props and how you used them. It's important that you don't gesture with a pen that is in one hand for the two-shot, and then have it jump to the other hand in the close up. It is likely that no one would notice it until they were in the editing room trying to put the shots together. Then it would be too late, and they would have to edit around — or not use — that take.

Therefore, if you use something like a cup or a pen in a scene, know where it travels to and from, and how you used it. Then be consistent from take to take.

On commercial shoots, if you handle the product itself, you will hear it referred to as the "hero." Often, these are prototypes, handmade especially for a commercial that is being shot before the product is in mass production. Even if the product is in production, the prop people will have done something to make the one you are using "camera ready," and they will be very concerned about what happens to their "hero." On industrial film shoots and commercial shoots with small budgets, it will be up to you and a production assistant to keep an eye on what and how props are being used.

If you are booked on a spot involving the eating of food, you will need to be aware of a special term, "the spit bucket." Sounds gross, I know, but I'll give you some illustrations. I did a commercial for a chain of steak restaurants, and during the afternoon I "ate" about fifteen entire steaks in order to get a good selection of takes of me biting and enjoying the food. Needless to say, I could not eat that much and, in fact, I didn't swallow any of it. There was a small bucket right next to my chair.

Just last week, we did a spot for a new potato chip. In one scene, we were to take just one chip off the top of a bowl and eat it. For about the first dozen takes we just chewed up the chip and swallowed it. But, it was right after we had eaten lunch, so we asked for some cups to spit into. It seemed to mildly irritate the production assistant who had to find the cups for us, but even the children in the spot were getting sick of the chips, and asking for a "spit bucket" was completely appropriate.

Show business is funny sometimes, and people will ask you to do all kinds of things without regard for your well-being or comfort. I always think you should go the extra mile, if possible. But don't hesitate to make sensible requests if you feel at risk in the use of props, or anything else. Whether it's a spit bucket, or ear protection for very loud noises, like gunfire, the production people might not remember to look out for you. Let your own common sense and responsibility guide you.

Tricks of the Trade

The other opportunity that props present is a way to "cheat" on your lines. Learning your lines for a commercial is seldom a problem. The scripts are fairly short, sometimes you have no lines at all, or your lines are on a TelePrompTer. Plus, commercials will be broken up into many short scenes, with lots of rehearsal and many takes. Finally, the language in commercials is usually "normal," words that you use every day.

Industrial films are another matter. The producer is often still revising the script when you arrive on the set, and you will be delivering much longer passages, often with technical or esoteric language. Memorizing some of these scripts is not easy. I have felt great sympathy as I watched an actor break into a cold sweat trying to remember some complex statistical information or computer jargon. The whole production can grind to a halt. Using a TelePrompTer (or earprompter, if you have one) is not always possible or practical, and yet you still have to find a way to deliver statistics, unfamiliar names, and those strange acronyms.

So, there are a few things that I nearly always take along for industrial film shoots: "props" that might be appropriate for a business setting. At the top of that list are a pen and a legal pad. Art direction on many industrial films is often fairly informal, and directors are usually amenable to your having pieces of script, or "notes," on a legal pad as a part of the set decoration. These are logical props for a desk or office setting, and if you can speed the shoot along by having little notes around to jog your memory on a difficult section of the script, then everyone is happy.

Scissors and tape are next on the list. I have been known to cut up a script and tape a particularly difficult phrase in some unseen place. Several times, when the camera was behind me shooting the other actor speaking to me, I held a piece of script in front of my face, just out of frame, for the other actor to read from as he or she delivered a difficult section.

In no way am I suggesting that you rely on any of these tricks to replace memorizing the script properly. However, sometimes at the end — or even in the middle of — a long day, speed becomes the priority, and you are expected to be able to come up with the lines one way or another, even if they are lines that have just been rewritten.

This is more a technique than a trick, but when you are being shot over the shoulder (OTS) of an actor to whom you are speaking, don't look from eye to eye, as we do in real life. It doesn't look right on camera. Look only into one eye of your fellow actor, the one closest to the shoulder over which the camera is focused. If you look from eye to eye, you appear to be looking away from the person.

If you are speaking with another actor in a two-shot, and it seems appropriate for pacing, you can overlap your lines with the other actor's. However (and this is usually the case), if you know that the director will be cutting back and forth between lines, be careful not to overlap your lines with the other actor's. It doesn't always feel natural or conversational, but the editor will need a tiny space between lines to make a clean edit. If you are in doubt, just ask the director if you need to leave some room between lines. Your awareness will be appreciated.

Ethics

"Ethics in the workplace" is a fairly hot topic these days. We believe that you will serve *yourself* best with ethical behavior in this business, and with ethical treatment of those with whom you work. Professionalism will be remembered. You will get a call from someone two years later who remembers not just your ability, but also your good work ethic — how you helped the shoot go more smoothly. A few themes recur throughout the comments of the producers and directors in Chapter 6, such as always being on time, but there are a few things worth under-scoring in the area of ethics.

When you are offered an audition, you will sometimes be told when the job shoots. If you know for sure that you are not available to work on that day, tell them. Sometimes the shoot date is just a maybe, and they will tell you to audition anyway. But if you go "just to be seen," hoping they will remember you for later, you waste their time and yours. Plus, you take up the space of an actor who is available, because they usually only see a certain number of people for each role. So, if they do want to book you, and it turns out that you never were available, you can be sure that they *will* remember you later.

If you can ice skate really well, or you have some special skill, by all means put it on your résumé. However, actors frequently tell one an-other to say "yes," no matter what it is that you are asked to do, on the theory that you will be able to learn before the job. If you say you can do something when you can't, you are begging for headaches. You can hold up a production, embarrass yourself, and make a very bad name for yourself in general. I was once asked if I could ice skate for an IRS in-dustrial film. I was honest and told them that I had skated only three times. They said that all I had to do was to speak and then skate out of frame. I got the job, practiced a lot, and the job went fine. Another time, I was asked if I had any mountain-climbing experience. It was a role that I was perfect for, and the job was mine if I said I could climb. But, I get nervous on tall ladders, and no amount of practice would make me into a climber. Why harm my reputation in the long run just to book one job? I told them they should not consider me. Later, they called me again, when there were no mountains involved.

Don't "crash" auditions. Some actors, who have more nerve than I, will try to get into an audition for which they were not scheduled. They are not just young actors trying to get started, either. We knew one woman, experienced, who was sure she was right for a project, so she went to where she knew the audition was happening and signed in. This is not difficult to do; commercial auditions in New York seem fairly anonymous at times. A casting assistant usually just calls the name of the next person who has signed in. But, the casting agent knew exactly whom she had called for the audition. She called the agent of our friend and chewed out the agent, even though he had nothing to do with it. Our friend almost lost her agent because of her actions.

Just last week, I was waiting to audition for an NBC prime-time police drama, and I watched as an actor tried to talk his way into the audition. The casting agent accepted his photo, studied it, and turned him away. That particular casting agent accepts photos by mail only, and has a sign on her door to make sure people know. In fact, I got the audition by mailing her my photo. The actor who tried to talk his way in will now be passed over if he does mail in his picture. She studied his photo to make sure she would remember him.

If all of this makes the casting people seem overly petty or mean, they aren't. It is a business — a business in which things usually happen on very tight schedules. If you waste, or unnecessarily take up, someone's time, then they fall behind in their schedule. One day of shooting can cost anywhere between $10,000 and $100,000 or more. Even a few minutes are worth measurable amounts of money.

So, if you save time for those you work with, by having a high work ethic, solid preparation, and good cooperation, they remember. If you waste their time, they remember. It is no different than any other business; people who make the job go smoother get noticed. Ironically, those people may not be the "stars," but they do build careers.

The good news, for people breaking into the business, is that the business needs you. So, even though behaving ethically by not crashing auditions and by telling the truth on your résumé might seem to cut you out of the process from time to time, there are systems in place for you to get seen. Periodicals like the *Ross Reports* in New York City (see Appendix C) spell out exactly how agents and casting people want to be contacted. In some places, there are agents that have an "open call" to meet new people. A little networking and legwork on your part, and your phone will eventually ring.

Other Mediums

Print Work
In most markets, commercial and industrial film work overlap with one another: the same agents, same casting people, same talent. But there

are several other types of "acting" work that accompany these two areas and can become specialties of their own. Print work, voice work, and "parts" modeling present ample opportunities for actors in commercial advertising and film work. The marketing of these skills differ from one another, and also from city to city. But there is no reason that you can't cross over into one or more of these specialties.

This section reaches outside our immediate topic of commercials and corporate films. But, work in one area will often lead to work in another, and we want you to be aware of all of the possibilities in these connected fields.

Ironically, in New York City, where there are the most opportunities, it often seems difficult to cross into other acting specialties, simply because of the number of actors, I suppose. But, don't let that hold you back. You may have to work with a different agent for each type of work, but if you have ability or desire in one area or another, pursue it. The more you can branch out, the better potential living you can make.

Print work, usually referred to as "print modeling," may be the most accessible of these other specialties, and it offers tremendous opportunities. Open a magazine to one of the numerous advertisements, or look at the photo on the box of some product you recently purchased, and you are looking at the results of a "print job." Entry into this field is simple: it only requires that you put together a "composite card," a standard format collection of photos of you in different "looks." The photos can be from previous print jobs, or posed to appear as though they might be from a job. Three composite card printers we have worked with are:

1. Super Shots. Los Angeles. (213) 724-4809.
2. MC Prints. New York City. (212) 337-3400.
3. ABC Pictures. Springfield, Missouri. (417) 869-9433.

Photographers love to work with "actors" on print jobs because most of these photos are, in fact, little acting scenes. But, I have worked with retired military personnel, Amtrak conductors, and school teachers who were using print work as an entry into the on-camera career they desired. Of course, the reality is that the talent on these jobs are referred to as "models," and tall and beautiful people are common in this specialty. But, by *no* means are all models tall and beautiful. Look through some of the magazines. If you see someone like yourself in any of the ads, then there might be a place for you in print modeling.

There are some other realities to print modeling. It can be very tedious work, you have to provide the wardrobe on many jobs, and you might not be paid right away. Usually, you are paid after the photographer gets paid, and the photographer usually doesn't bill for the job until the finished product is ready. So, ninety days is common between job and paycheck. But, on an hourly basis, you are looking at doctor's wages. So, a print job now and then can be a very nice bonus on top of your other acting jobs.

If you have little in the way of photographs that would be usable on a comp card, talk to some of your fellow actors and try to find a commercial photographer who does "test" shots. When photographers are trying to build their own portfolio, they sometimes shoot test shots of different models in various situations. You are then paid for your work with copies of the prints. Or, if you can afford to do so, you can hire a photographer whose business is to help models put together portfolio shots. These photographers advertise in trade papers like *Backstage* (see Appendix C), or you could ask a reputable talent agent who handles print work for suggestions of photographers. However, NEVER pay a company promoting itself as a "talent agency" to put together a portfolio for you (see the "Scams" section, Chapter 8).

Many agencies, when they take an interest in working with you, will want to have a hand in choosing the photographs that will be on your card. If so, welcome their input because they know the market and what will sell. They might also know printers that do better or cheaper cards, or that have the agency's logo on file to print on your card.

Everyone has limits on what they can spend to promote themselves, but don't choose your printer just because they are cheap. A photographer will hire a model just from looking through a stack of these cards. A cheap-looking card will make an implied statement about your ability, and will probably just be a waste of your money. If possible, ask a local agent if you can see what current cards look like, to get some ideas. We have been doing this for some time, and we still check out what other people are doing before we put together a new comp card.

Voice Work

Voice work includes a very large area of work: voice-over (indicated as VO on scripts) for commercials and films, narrations on industrial films and documentary films, announcers on commercials and radio and TV shows, audiobook recordings, and radio commercials. It can get quite specialized even within the general category, and you will need to have an audio demo reel, because a high percentage of these jobs are booked from reels. There are auditions for voices or announcers on many new ad campaigns, but you will need a reel to get an agent to send you on the audition. This sounds like a catch-22, I know, but — just like with comp cards — you can hire someone to help you put together a reel if this is a new area for you.

In most areas, there are voice coaches or sound engineers who advertise their services and who can help you put together material for a reel. Again, check the trade papers, and get on the mailing list of a local actors' affiliation. You will find people there who can guide you. Ask around and check out their reputations before you spend a lot of money. There are many people selling actors' services, but not all of them have something worth buying.

If you have a potential for voice work, you probably already know it. You have a deep, rich, clear voice, or you can do character voices. If you are one of these people, there will always be work for you; you just have to get your tapes out. But, as for the rest of us, listen to radio commercials and to the voice-overs of television spots, and you will notice that, just like with on-camera work, producers are hiring a lot more "regular" or "interesting" voices. It is no longer the typical "announcer" voice on every spot. There is usually a dynamic quality or some "edge" in the voice, but again, your own desire will guide you here.

The keys to good voice work, besides a good or interesting voice, are exaggeration and perfect timing. Without the rest of your body to tell the story, your words must convey the meaning that would otherwise be in your eyes and face.

In some ways, this is harder than acting with your whole body. But, there is a great trick. When you are recording your voice, for a job or for practice, *use your hands*. It seems funny, but it works. For instance, if you have to say the word *enormous*, use your hands to draw a big ball in the air as you say the word, and your voice will be more expressive. Needless to say, put a *big* smile on your face if the copy needs to be upbeat, or if you are saying words like *happy*. Of course, you can't make any noise with your gestures, or the microphone will pick it up, but you will find that involving your body in *exaggerated* gestures will help fill your voice with the life and imagery that it needs. Don't feel self-conscious about it; the sound engineer sees this all the time.

As for timing, get a stopwatch and practice. This will help you with on-camera delivery as well. Industrial films rarely need for a scene to be delivered in a predetermined length of time, but TV and radio spots all have to fit precisely into a time slot: twelve seconds, eighteen seconds, twenty-seven seconds, etc. The copywriter will usually be pretty good about writing copy that will fit into the planned time period, but if there are too many words, or too few words, you have to make them fit. Start off practicing with a piece of copy to see if you can do it in the same time several times in a row. Then try trimming off one second.

To trim off a couple of seconds, you will need to pick up the energy of the whole piece. If you want to trim small amounts of time, like a half second, then read the piece the same way as you have been doing, but pick up the pace of the last phrase just a little, or the last two phrases, if needed. You will be surprised how, with some practice, you can deliver the copy consistently in the exact time you want.

It's good to get some practice at this, just to know that you can do it. Believe me, when you are new at doing this, you can break out in a sweat when the producer tells you, "That was perfect! It just needs to be three-quarters of a second shorter." But then it's fun when you are able to trim off exactly that much.

Parts Modeling

Another category of work for you to consider is "parts modeling." Look carefully at print ads and television commercials and you will see lots of shots that have only a hand showing, using the product. It is easier to notice these shots in print ads. With TV commercials, your mind connects the hand to the body in the previous scene, or you watch the product, which is exactly what you are supposed to do. But, nearly all of these scenes that include just the hand, or some other body part, are shot separately, and usually with a "hand model." In New York City and Los Angeles, there are talent agencies that specialize in handling parts models. You can find them listed in the *Ross Reports* (see Appendix C).

Most people are aware, from various movies about the topic, that just as there are "stunt doubles" who handle the dangerous scenes for various actors, there are also "body doubles" who take over in a nude scene, or who double for the actor in a scene where the face doesn't show. If the scene calls for Tom Cruise to be walking in the distance down a Washington street, they don't really need Tom. He can be in Hollywood, looping the sound, or in his hotel, sleeping. Nor do they need Tom, or his costar, in that steamed-up shower. That's where you can take over.

Squire Fridell, in his book *Acting in Television Commercials for Fun and Profit,* and whose face you know very well from his Toyota ads and many other spots, talks about how he kept his teaching job long after he was making a good living in commercials. It gave him something to do when he wasn't acting, and, more important, it put him in the position of not "needing" the jobs for which he was auditioning. "Neediness" erodes your abilities and your confidence. So, the less that you put all of your eggs in one basket, the better chance you have over the long term.

The other advantage in pursuing commercials and industrials and print work and voice work and stage work and whatever else interests you, is that, in their own way, each is an acting job, and the best way to become a better actor is to act. So, posing for a print job doesn't just put a little more money in your pocket; it can make you a better actor.

Acting on-camera will benefit your other acting pursuits in another very positive way if you truly learn on-camera acting's greatest lesson: "If you *think real thoughts,* it will be in your eyes, and if it is in your eyes, it will be in your body."

8

Show "Business"

It may be only a slight exaggeration to say that if you choose to attend a four-year university for training as an actor, you won't be taught even the basics of what is contained in this chapter. Acting schools are in the business of teaching you how to act, which is great. However, we want to teach you how to *work* as an actor.

For an actor, auditioning and working on-camera is a highly intense, emotional experience. But, for most of the other professionals in the business, it is just that — a business. Most of the people you will meet in your pursuit of acting work have an office and a business card, and they get up and go to work on a schedule every day. Missing from their experience are the emotional highs and lows that can drive us to excellence, or drive us crazy.

The casting professionals you will meet spend much of their day wrestling with budgets and faxes and negotiations. You have to blend your passion, drive, and talent with their need to get the job done.

If you are to achieve success as an actor over the long run, someone will have to manage your career in a businesslike fashion, whether it's you, or your mate, or your manager, or your agent. "Treat this as a business" is a persistent theme in the agent/director/producer comments we reprinted in Chapter 6. Practicing good business skills won't necessarily get you a specific job, but it will absolutely get you more auditions and more opportunities, which, over time, will get you more jobs.

Some of what we suggest in this area might seem obvious, but our experience is that most people who are new to the business — and many of those who have struggled for years — don't understand the relationship between respect for the business aspects and personal success.

The good news is that most of this is simple to do, and we promise you that it will make your life easier and your career more successful.

Our Top Ten Business Suggestions

1. Always Be on Time.

2. Always Send a Cover Letter and Résumé.

When you send your headshot to someone, always send a brief cover letter explaining why you have sent them your photo. You may think the reason is obvious, but they can't know what you want if you don't tell them. Also, always attach your résumé to the back of the photo. If your unattached résumé gets separated from the photo, they don't know who you are, or how to contact you. The résumé should be trimmed to size and should have your current contact numbers, but not your address.

Your cover letter should be addressed to a specific person. Look up the agency in the *Ross Reports* and pick the name of an appropriate person, or call them and ask their policy on submissions, and to whom you can send a photo.

Your letter should be polite and very short, something like:

Dear Ms. Smith,

I'm new to (the area) and seeking representation. I don't have a long résumé, but I have good training and much desire.

I look forward to meeting you personally and working with you. I can be reached at 800-555-1212.

Sincerely,

(or . . .)

Dear Mr. Jones,

I understand that you cast for commercials and industrial films. Please consider me on the next project that calls for someone of my type.

I can be reached at 800-555-1212, and look forward to auditioning for you.

Sincerely,

3. Keep Good Records.

Write everything in a calendar book or journal, or on a pad secured by the phone. Notes on the back of the nearest envelope will get lost, and you won't make a good impression by calling people to tell them that you lost the audition information and need them to give it to you again. You might even forget a meeting with someone because you failed to write it where you could find it.

When you have an appointment, write down a phone number where you can call in case you have some unforeseen problem on the way and have to be late.

If you don't have a great memory, keep notes in your book on people you meet, along with pertinent information. You'll be surprised how impressed people are when you "remember" details about them when you see them again. Plus, you will have more to talk about in that next meeting: "How did your son do at that swim meet?"

4. Have an Answering Machine or Voice Mail with a Short, Businesslike Message.

You may feel your long musical parody or comedy routine is funny but it will only be funny the first time they call, and probably not even then. They call a lot of machines.

5. Return Calls Promptly.

Two hours should be the limit on getting back to people. If you don't have Call Waiting get it, or even better, consider getting Call Answering. With this service, your voicemail box picks up when you are on the phone, so you don't have to put people on hold.

Most of all, be reachable.

6. Send Thank-You Notes.

Send brief notes to thank people for seeing you, or casting you, or to stay in touch with new information about yourself. Gifts are almost never appropriate as a way to say "thank you." If you feel that a gift is appropriate as a way of saying "thanks," keep it modest so you don't embarrass them. Send a box of Girl Scout cookies, or a little cactus plant — not two dozen roses.

7. Be Ready.

Keep your wardrobe and personal grooming up to date and ready. Current, clean, conservative wardrobe choices are best. You don't have to spend a lot of money. You can often find great business suits and evening wear at consignment stores. Your wardrobe should be consistent with the local market, and with your type. New York, Los Angeles, Washington, D.C., and many other cities have very individual looks (conservative, sporty, urban) but a banker or an attorney or a casual mom are going to look pretty much the same everywhere (at least on-camera).

Keep your wardrobe where you can find it and in ready-to-go condition, for those last-minute jobs or auditions.

8. Make Sure Your Headshot Looks Like You.

This is a mistake made by many. If you decide to change your hair from brunette to blond, or grow a full beard, you need to update your photo. Many producers have been burned by hiring someone from a photo, only to find out the actor had changed hair colors, gone bald, or gained forty pounds. You will always score points with a decent headshot that *looks like you*.

9. Be Willing and Open to Helping Others.

Some of your best information will come through networking, by exchanging information with other willing actors. This is one of the only businesses that you can enter successfully at any age and remain actively involved in for as long as you want. You'll meet amazing people, and they will be amazed by you, too.

10. Always Be on Time!

Agents and Managers

Although there can be some crossover, managers and agents generally perform very different functions for an actor. Managers seem to exist mostly in New York City and Los Angeles, where competition is most fierce.

An agent is the go-between for you (the actor) and casting people, producers, or directors. The agent is, in a sense, like an employment counselor, looking for job openings and then trying to match people that he or she represents to those jobs. They exist in almost every market in the country, and are an essential ingredient in your career.

Managers, in theory, take a much more personal interest in guiding and counseling you and your career, seeking individual opportunities especially for you. An agent might get you and ten other clients an audition for a project, along with all the other people from other agencies. A manager, on the other hand, might get you a meeting with the producer of the project.

For their specialized services, managers then will sign you to a contract that entitles them to at least 15 percent of *everything* that you make, whether they find you the job or not. The agent will generally collect 10 percent only on the work you booked through that agent, depending on the contract you may have with that agent.

We feel that managers are only appropriate for three categories of actors: children; highly successful celebrity-status actors, who need help with managing their time and finding or coordinating projects; and actors who are fairly new to the business and who have much potential in the highly competitive markets of New York City and Los Angeles. This last category is the hardest to define, but I have known some very talented young people who, thanks to their manager, got through lots of otherwise-closed doors in Hollywood, and now have their own TV series. Unfortunately, I have also known actors who did not get much benefit from their managers, but still had to pay them for all the jobs that they found on their own. This is where your own judgment, and the asking of many questions, will have to guide you.

You should be aware that, unlike most talent agents, managers are not regulated by any of the performers' unions, or by anyone else, for that matter. Legitimate managers will not *promise* you any employment, and they do not advertise or otherwise solicit through the mail, in malls, or anywhere else. Once again, word of mouth and networking are how you will know about the good ones.

Agents, on the other hand, are necessary and useful to every actor. We considered printing a list of all of the union-franchised agents in the country, but a list like that would be out of date by the time you got this book. However, up-to-date lists can be obtained from a local SAG/AFTRA office, or from the *Ross Reports* (see Appendix C).

Some agents are not franchised by a union. This doesn't mean they aren't good; it just means they work on nonunion projects. Franchised agents can only work on union projects, or they lose their franchise. But, you will never find a legitimate agent, franchised or not, listing their services in a newspaper ad or any other kind of advertisement. The one exception to that would be if an agent needed a *huge* number of people for some scene in a movie or commercial.

In general, you will meet potential agents either by sending them your headshot and getting a call from them, or by attending an "open call" held by that agent. When you send out your headshot, be organized about it. If you are in New York City or Los Angeles, target your mailings to agents appropriate for what you want to do, and send a limited number at a time, with follow-up postcards or notes later. A mass mailing to every agent in town wastes money, and if you get a big response, you won't be able to keep up.

I hear actors refer to agents in somewhat adversarial terms, and actors are forever "firing" their agents, when they are not happy with their careers. With many actors, there is a kind of built-in suspicion of agents, and I often hear them say, "He's working for *you*, not the other way around!" or, "Why didn't your agent get you in on that?" But the best relationships between agents and actors are mutually respecting. In the end, you both have the same goal: for you to make money.

When you meet or deal with agents, keep in mind that they are exactly like you. They have rent to pay, dogs to feed, and bosses to please. On top of that, everyone wants something from them. Agents have told us stories of actors trying to hand them a résumé while the agent was in a bathroom stall.

Finding an agent with whom you can successfully work can be a challenge. However, making that all-important good "first impression" is often as simple as treating them as you would want to be treated.

Communicate respectfully. Use last names until they suggest otherwise. Listen to them. Be as warm and friendly as possible, and do not bring any personal baggage with you into the meeting. Just like you, they will respond to someone with a good attitude. Find topics that are mutually interesting, and try to forget the idea of "what they can do for you."

A relationship with an agent that is based on respect and mutual concern will last longer and serve the goals of both parties involved.

Scams

Acting is a great profession. If you have a passion for it, you can make your living doing something you love, and it can take you all over the country, or even the world. Even if you just pursue acting part-time, you can get great pleasure from a business that allows you to "play" for a living.

Perhaps because so many people dream of doing this, there are a lot of scam artists out there who promise to get you into the business quicker—if you just give them a lot of money. It's true in real estate, and it's true in acting: "Buyer beware!"

We can point out some of the most prevalent scams, but it is up to you to keep your eyes open. We think this book can help you immensely, but by no means will we tell you that if you only read this book, you are ready for a career in the business. You should read the other books, take classes, study on your own, practice, observe, organize, pursue. And always keep your "intellect" fully engaged, as an actor and as a consumer.

We have already mentioned a few of the ways that people will try to separate you from your money, but they are worth repeating. The most common is bogus "talent" agencies. If an "agency" advertises—in the newspaper, on TV, or anywhere—you should be suspicious. Legitimate agents don't need to advertise to attract people. Most of these companies that advertise are really in the business of selling you photographs—usually not very good ones and always at too high a price. They will tell you something like, "We think you have potential, but we need to shoot a 'test' shot of you." They will charge you a fee for the test shot. If they think that test shot is good (and they'll think so, believe me), they will want you to shoot real photos—with their photographer, of course. Then, they will want to print them for you. Hundreds of dollars later, you probably won't have very much that is actually usable. Real agencies will suggest photographers, but they won't charge you any money for anything. As a rule, if an agency wants any money for anything, leave.

Of course, there are exceptions, but they make sense. I know of one agency that needed a couple of thousand extras for a movie. They placed an ad in the paper, and each person that responded was charged $2.00 for a Polaroid photo. That is what a Polaroid costs. Two dollars, not sixty.

If an agency has a school, be suspicious, especially if they suggest that if you take their classes, they will get you work. If they have a school, that is probably how they really make their money, and you will probably pay a high price for inferior training. There are exceptions here, too, but speak to someone who has taken their training. If an acting school implies that they can get you a job as an actor, you should be suspicious. You get jobs in this business by auditioning, or by requests from people who already know your work. That is true whether you are just starting out or whether you are already a big "star."

Of course, even legitimate agencies aren't beyond making an extra buck here and there. They might have a line of T-shirts. Lots of agents put together print books, and ask the models to pay the cost of printing their own photos in the book. But, these are marketing devices, and you won't even be asked to be in the book unless they already know you.

Many agencies are putting together CD-ROM of their talent. It remains to be seen how effective these will be, but again, if they don't even know you and still want to sell you a space on their CD, think long and hard about it.

If you do investigate a school for on-camera training, the primary question should be, "How much time will I spend on-camera?" The most effective place to learn is in front of a camera, where you can see a replay of what you are doing and then improve it.

Most cities of any size have various "hotlines" for actors to call, sponsored by one of the actors' unions or a local actors' coalition. Those are always good sources of information.

Our feeling is that you should check out everything that interests you, but keep your hand on your wallet. Some things that seem unlikely turn out fine.

I remember seeing an ad in the paper for an "open call" in Washington, D.C., for the Broadway musical *Les Misérables*. Being the "big shot" that I am, with Broadway musical credits and all, I was sure this was — if not an actual scam — at least just a publicity stunt to sell tickets for the show. After all, Broadway shows audition in New York, right? One of our students went to the "open call," got a callback, was flown to New York to meet the director, and was in the national tour two weeks later.

Just balance your willingness with a healthy amount of caution, and you'll be fine.

Unions

The unions for professional actors are Screen Actors Guild (SAG), and American Federation of Television and Radio Artists (AFTRA). There is quite a bit of crossover coverage, and it's possible that SAG and AFTRA may have merged by the time you read this book. As a rule, however, SAG has jurisdiction over the majority of commercials and all feature films, and AFTRA covers radio work, television shows, and some corporate films and commercials (depending on which market you are in). Actors' Equity Association has jurisdiction over all professional stage work, and some live industrial shows. Opera and cabaret also have their own unions.

I certainly know people who work as actors on nonunion projects. They get great enjoyment, and they make fairly good money. Probably, if you are just starting out, you should do as much nonunion work as you can afford to do, just for the experience. But, eventually, if you are enjoying any success, joining the proper union will be in your best interest.

The trade papers, such as *Backstage*, list auditions by category of union or nonunion, and you will see that there are lots of jobs in both categories.

But, for some jobs, you will have no choice, and you will have to join a union. The catch-22 is that to be in the union you must first book a union job — but you can't audition for many of these jobs unless you are already in the union. However, lawsuits involving "equal access" have opened more opportunities, especially with stage work.

Many years ago, Congress passed the Taft-Hartley Law, which applies to union membership. Among other things, it provides for a person to be able to do at least one job under a union jurisdiction without having to join the union. There are time limitations, and the law is applied with some variations, but in general, it provides that you can work for a thirty-day period without joining, or you may work in place of a union member if you fill a special need that is not available within the union ranks.

In most cases, you will become a "must join" after that first job, or after a certain time period if you want to continue working on union-affiliated jobs. I think being a union member gives you a certain credibility as a professional. It guarantees certain salaries and working conditions, and it opens up possibilities for you. For instance, union-affiliated talent agencies cannot and will not work with anyone who is not in the union already, or who is willing to join at the first opportunity.

Joining the union is a very personal decision, and you should not necessarily rush into it. But, for a union actor, salaries and working conditions are generally very good, and the contracts, along with residual payment schedules, are prenegotiated and enforced by the union.

Once you have decided you are willing to join a union, the problem becomes how to get that first job to qualify you for membership. Join when you can and when you want to, but don't be held back either way. Years ago, I sang in a group called the Heymakers at the Country Dinner Playhouse in Dallas. We warmed up the audience before the show. One of our members was Pat Richardson. She wanted to go to New York City, so she left the group. I wondered how she would ever get a job, since she didn't belong to any of the unions. Well, I was naïve, and she was talented. The next time I saw her she was playing the wife across from Tim Allen in a new show on TV called "Home Improvement."

Information about membership in Screen Actors Guild, along with other valuable information about actors' services in your area, can be obtained by calling the office nearest you (see Appendix E for a list).

9

Final Thoughts

Early in 1997, I was called in to audition for the part of a newspaper editor in an episode of the NBC television series "Homicide: Life on the Street." I was to read for John Strawbridge of Pat Moran Casting. I had been given pages of a scene, but no real description of the character. Before auditioning, I told John what my idea was for the part, and I asked him if I was heading in the right direction. His response was wonderful, and it pretty much boiled down to one sentence the whole concept of on-camera acting: "Well, we've had several different interpretations, but it's not wrong unless it's not believable."

People will tell you that auditioning, and even the business as a whole, is a competition. One person wins and everybody else loses. But we encourage you not to view it that way. Yes, it is very competitive, and yes, when you don't book a job that you auditioned for, it sometimes feels like you lost. But, when you do well at an audition you will be remembered, and that will lead to other auditions. Even if you do poorly at an audition, don't beat yourself up about it. You will learn from that how to improve the next one, and the communication skills you gain from this business will serve you for life, in everything you do.

In class, we tell people that there isn't a right way to do this; there's only *your* way. Your interpretation — your vision of the character — is as valid as any other actor's.

Don't hold back.

Follow your instincts.

Be bold.

Appendix A
Practice Copy

We chose a selection of practice copy that not only includes a good variety but, with a little imagination, could be done by anyone. In other words, it may be written for a "Mom" or "Husband and Wife," but you can practice it as a "Dad" or "Sisters." It may be an industrial narration written for a female news anchor type, but could be done by a male or a typical employee of the company.

Some of the pieces are humorous. You may not see yourself as a comic type, but some of the best comedy results from giving "straight" actors (noncomedy types) something funny to say. The result is something other than what we expect, which can be funny all by itself. So, try all of the copy.

If you can practice with your home camera, so much the better, but don't wait until you can set up equipment. You really only need your imagination.

With each piece, do the following, and mark the copy to help you remember the things you have in mind.

1. Picture, in your imagination, "where you are," and do so in great detail.
2. Know what your character is doing in the instant before the dialogue or scene begins, and also in the moment after it ends. Remember that with the exception of "hard" narrations, these are all little moments of life in progress, and even the narration has to take place somewhere. You need to imagine where that place might be.
3. Look for places to find humor in all of the copy, places you can add a laugh or smile. Find ways to lighten the pieces, especially the copy that doesn't seem humorous, like pain-reliever ads and business interview situations.

Commercial Copy

Gum

I'M CHEWING GUM AGAIN. IT'S WONDERFUL! FOR YEARS I COULDN'T BECAUSE GUM STUCK TO MY DENTAL WORK. BUT NOW THERE'S DENTIFREE GUM. IT DOESN'T STICK! SO I CAN ENJOY ALL THE PLEASURES OF CHEWING GUM AGAIN. THE DELICIOUS FLAVOR . . . FRESH CLEAN BREATH . . . AND REFRESHING TASTE. ALL THAT'S POSSIBLE AGAIN . . . WITH DENTIFREE. TRY IT IN PEPPERMINT AND NEW SPEARMINT. DENTIFREE GUM . . . YOU'LL LOVE IT.

Pizza

I LOVE FAST FOOD. . . . AND I LOVE HAMBURGERS AND CHICKEN. . . . BUT SOMETIMES I NEED A CHANGE . . . SOMETHING DIFFERENT. THAT'S WHEN I HEAD FOR THE PIZZA PLACE. REGULAR, OR NEW DEEP-DISH PIZZA FROM THE PIZZA PLACE. . . . DECIDEDLY DIFFERENT . . . DEFINITELY DELICIOUS!

Pain Relief

SOMETIMES A HEADACHE AT NIGHT WILL GET ME SO TENSE, THAT BETWEEN THE PAIN, AND THE TENSION, I JUST CAN'T SLEEP! ENOUGH TO MAKE IT HARD TO LOOK GOOD THE NEXT MORNING. BUT THERE'S A PAIN RELIEVER THAT'S MADE FOR NIGHTTIME HEADACHES . . . EXTRA STRENGTH PM. IT RELIEVES THE HEADACHE AND ITS TENSION, AND GIVES YOU EXTRA HELP TO RELAX FOR A GOOD NIGHT'S SLEEP . . . SO YOU SHOULD WAKE UP FEELING FINE. TRY EXTRA STRENGTH PM. . . . 'CAUSE IN THE MORNING, YOU MAY ONLY LOOK AS GOOD AS YOU FEEL.

Pharmacy Chain
(Female, with lipstick. A male could say "My wife . . .")

I DECIDED TO TRY THIS HOT NEW COLOR, THAT ALL THE MAGAZINES ARE RAVING ABOUT . . .

SO, I GO TO SUPER SAVE AND PICK IT UP.

AHHH . . . IT'S HORRIBLE. ANOTHER ONE TO ADD TO THE MAKEUP JUNK DRAWER, RIGHT? *WRONG!* SUPER SAVE's GOT THIS NEW COSMETICS MONEY-BACK GUARANTEE . . . AND IT'S RISK FREE. YOU DON'T LIKE IT? . . . SUPER SAVE GIVES YOU YOUR MONEY BACK. WE ALL MAKE MISTAKES BUYING COSMETICS. BUT NOW . . . WE DON'T HAVE TO PAY FOR THEM.

Cookies

(Mom) . . . SOMEONE'S BEEN SNEAKING MY GENEVA COOKIES. (Looks at Son) . . . HIM? IS HE CAPABLE OF INDULGING HIMSELF THE WAY I DO? . . . THE BABY! . . . WOULD SHE KNOW HOW TO SAVOR EVERY MOMENT?

THE PLUMBER! . . . COULD HE POSSIBLY APPRECIATE? . . . NO.

Car Insurance

THIS ISN'T JUST A CAR. . . . IT'S A SIGN OF HOW FAR YOU'VE COME. SO, IF IT GETS DAMAGED, WHO DO YOU WANT ON YOUR SIDE?

AT COUNTRY-WIDE INSURANCE, WE GUARANTEE THAT YOUR CAR WILL BE FIXED, JUST THE WAY IT SHOULD BE . . . BECAUSE WE WOULDN'T HAVE IT ANY OTHER WAY.

Bank

(Reminder: Where are you? Try putting the character behind the wheel of a car, waiting for the next drive-up ATM. That will give you lots of choices for what to do before and after you speak.)

AMERICAN'S DRIVE-UP RESPONSE CENTERS SEEM INCREDIBLE. TO DO ALL YOUR BANKING WITHOUT GOING INSIDE THE BANK . . . FROM YOUR CAR . . . DEPOSITS, MONEY TRANSFERS, BALANCES, EVEN CASH 24 HOURS A DAY . . . FROM A MACHINE!

HOW DOES IT KNOW HOW TO DO ALL THAT? MAGIC? NO. THINK ABOUT IT. IT'LL HIT YOU. MINIATURE TELLERS. SITTING INSIDE THERE WITH MINIATURE CHAIRS, MINIATURE

CLOTHES. A MACHINE LIKE THIS COULD HOLD TEN . . . MAYBE TWELVE OF THEM. YUP . . . MINIATURE TELLERS. PROBABLY COME IN THROUGH A MINIATURE DOOR. IT'S ONLY LOGICAL.

(Another reminder: When you have a "laundry list" of product features—like with the list beginning with "DEPOSITS"—each item needs to be distinguished in some subtle way, with a change of inflection or new vocal attack. The second paragraph offers the comedy that will help the viewer remember the commercial, but the laundry list is what you are selling, and what the client wants to hear.)

Motel Chain

I TRAVEL TO OVER 100 CITIES A YEAR, AND THAT MEANS STAYING IN A LOT OF MOTELS . . . SO, WHEN WESTERN CHOICE ASKED ME TO BE THEIR SPOKESMAN . . . I WAS DELIGHTED.

I STAY IN THEM AND I CAN RECOMMEND THEM.

WESTERN CHOICE HAS OVER 90,000 ROOMS FROM COAST TO COAST, BUT I ALWAYS SAVE TIME BY CALLING AHEAD . . . USING THEIR TOLL-FREE NUMBER. IF YOU FORGET THEIR RESERVATION NUMBER, IT'S IN THE WHITE PAGES. WESTERN CHOICE . . . A *GREAT* PLACE TO STAY WHEN *YOU'RE* NOT AT HOME.

Fast-Food Chain

I'VE BEEN CHEATING ON MY WIFE. SEE, SHE PUTS ME ON THESE DIETS, BUT AFTER A FEW DAYS I SNEAK OFF AND GET A BURGER. I'D FEEL TERRIBLE . . . BUT NOW JACK'S HAS THIS NEW LEAN SIRLOIN BURGER. LESS THAN 15% FAT, BUT IT'S LOADED WITH GOODIES. IT'S NOT LIKE I'M SEEING ANOTHER WOMAN . . . I'M SEEING ANOTHER BURGER.

. . . SAME TIME TOMORROW?

Lottery

I LOVE THESE FAMILY GATHERINGS . . . AND BOY, DO I HAVE A LOT OF FAMILY! (Laughs) ESPECIALLY SINCE I WON THE

LOTTERY! (A bizarre, costumed man from the Old Country runs in and gives you a hug.) . . . COUSIN SCHEMNKE!!

DOESN'T SPEAK A WORK OF ENGLISH, BUT FOUND ME THE DAY AFTER I WON! AMAZING!

(Waves) AH . . . COUSIN MOHAMMED! COUSIN CHAN!

YOU KNOW, THE GREAT PART ABOUT WINNING ISN'T THE MONEY . . . IT'S MEETING ALL THE RELATIVES YOU NEVER KNEW YOU HAD.

Funeral Services

. . . IT WAS REALLY TOUGH WHEN MOM PASSED AWAY. DAD WASN'T IN THE BEST OF HEALTH . . . AND EVERYTHING FELL ON MY SHOULDERS. I'M REALLY THANKFUL THE FOLKS HERE AT THOMAS FUNERAL HOME WALKED ME THROUGH ALL THE ARRANGEMENTS . . . STEP BY STEP. THEY EVEN CONVINCED ME NOT TO SPEND QUITE AS MUCH AS I WAS TEMPTED TO.

CALL THEM . . . THEY'LL TAKE THE TIME TO SEE TO YOUR NEEDS PERSONALLY.

Cruise Ship Line

IMAGINE THE EXCITEMENT OF VISITING THE SEAPORTS OF SPANISH PIRATES . . . IMAGINE WALKING ON COBBLESTONE STREETS OVER FOUR HUNDRED YEARS OLD . . . IMAGINE LUXURIOUS, DUTY-FREE SHOPPING, AND MILES OF SILKY WHITE-SAND BEACHES . . .

THEN, PICTURE YOURSELF HAVING SEVEN DAYS OF REST AND RELAXATION ON A SUNRISE CARRIBEAN CRUISE.

YOU'LL SAIL FROM MIAMI. ALL OF YOUR FOOD, DRINKS, AND ENTERTAINMENT ARE INCLUDED IN YOUR ONE, LOW, SUNRISE PRICE . . . AND RATES START AT LESS THAN $400 PER PERSON.

IF THAT SOUNDS GOOD TO YOU, CALL YOUR TRAVEL AGENT . . . OR SUNRISE CARIBBEAN CRUISE . . . THE CARIBBEAN ADVENTURE!

Computer Services

(Looking at computer screen)

Guy 1: WWW.COM . . . CHECK THIS OUT.

Guy 2: WHAT MAKES THE LOGO ROTATE LIKE THAT? . . . COOL!

Guy 1: CHECK THIS OUT . . . IT'S FULLY RENDERED.

Guy 2: I LIKE THAT.

Guy 1: OOOH . . . LOOK!

Both: AHH . . . YEAH . . . YES . . . (etc.)

Guy 2: WE COULD GET A FLAMING, DANCING LOGO.

Guy 1: WE CAN DO ANYTHING!

Guy 2: CAN YOU ORDER ANY OF THIS STUFF?

Guy 1: . . . NO. . . . CUSTOM-WEB DESIGNED THIS . . . WE USE SOMEBODY ELSE.

Newspaper

Joe: HI, DENISE . . . GOOD WEEKEND?

Denise: OKAY . . . SAW A GREAT SHOW OFF-BROADWAY, RAN A 5K SATURDAY MORNING, WENT TO THE AUTO SHOW, A RENAISSANCE FESTIVAL . . .

Joe: I MISSED THE 5K . . . HOW DID YOU KNOW . . . ?

Denise: (Hides her copy of the *Times*) . . . JUST PAYIN' ATTEN-TION, JOE . . .

V/O: "The *Times* Weekend Section . . . now you can plan your weekend before it starts."

Denise: WHAT DID YOU DO?

Joe: I READ THE *POST*.

Health Services

Wife: HOW LONG HAS IT BEEN SINCE YOU'VE SEEN A DOCTOR?

Husband: THERE'S NOTHING WRONG WITH ME.

Wife: FIVE YEARS? TEN YEARS?

Husband: I'M PERFECTLY HEALTHY. WHY SEE A DOCTOR IF YOU'RE NOT SICK?

Wife: MAKES SENSE TO ME. WHY CHANGE THE OIL IF THE CAR STILL RUNS?

Husband: ANYWAY, WE'RE WAY TOO BUSY AT WORK.

Wife: YOUR FATHER USED TO SAY THAT. RIGHT UP TO THE DAY HE HAD HIS HEART ATTACK.

Political Spot

AS A PARENT, I'M CONCERNED ABOUT WHAT KIND OF PEOPLE LEAD OUR COMMUNITY. CALL ME OLD-FASHIONED, BUT CHARACTER MATTERS TO ME. AND THAT'S WHY I HAVE SOME REAL QUESTIONS ABOUT ANDY PARKER.

IT SAYS RIGHT HERE THAT PARKER WAS THE SUBJECT OF THREE SEPARATE INVESTIGATIONS INVOLVING LAND FRAUD. AND PARKER REFUSES TO EXPLAIN THE OFFICIAL COURT RECORDS SHOWING HE DIDN'T PAY CHILD SUP-PORT . . . IS THIS THE KIND OF PERSON WE WANT REPRE-SENTING OUR VIEWS . . . AND OUR VALUES?

Political Spot

BY NOW YOU'VE HEARD ALL THE ARGUMENTS FOR AND AGAINST THE NEW FUEL TAX. IF YOU'RE STILL UNDECIDED, HERE'S SOMETHING YOU MAY WANT TO KNOW.

THE PEOPLE SUPPORTING THE FUEL TAX SAY THEY NEED THE MONEY TO REPAIR UNSAFE BRIDGES AND CONSTRUCT NEW ROADS. THAT SOUNDS GOOD, BUT UNFORTUNATELY, IT'S NOT COMPLETELY TRUE.

FIRST OF ALL, THEY DON'T NEED THE MONEY. THE STATE HAS A 170 MILLION DOLLAR REVENUE SURPLUS FROM LAST YEAR, AND THE POLITICIANS BEHIND THIS TAX DON'T TELL YOU THAT NEXT YEAR, THEY HAVE THE POWER TO TAKE THIS MONEY AWAY FROM ROADS AND PUT IT INTO THE

GENERAL FUND, WHERE THEY CAN SPEND IT ANY WAY THEY WANT.

PLEASE DON'T BE INFLUENCED OR MANIPULATED BY MIS-LEADING EMOTIONAL APPEALS. THIS TAX IS NOT IN YOUR BEST INTEREST. I HOPE YOU'LL JOIN ME IN VOTING AGAINST THE NEW FUEL TAX.

Political Spot

Wife: YOU MEAN WE OWE MONEY?

Husband: YEAH. IT'S WORSE THAN I THOUGHT.

Wife: ANYTHING WE DIDN'T DEDUCT? WHAT ABOUT THE $500 TAX CREDIT FOR EACH OF OUR KIDS?

Husband: THE PRESIDENT VETOED IT. AND HE JOKED EVEN *HE* THINKS HE'S RAISED TAXES TOO MUCH!

Wife: HE HAS! THE PRESIDENT PROMISED US A TAX CUT. CONGRESS GIVES US ONE AND HE VETOES IT. HE DOESN'T GET IT . . . HE'S SPENDING OUR MONEY!

Corporate Film Copy

Host/Narration

INFORMATION SUPERHIGHWAY . . . INTERNET . . . WORLD WIDE WEB . . . MULTIMEDIA . . . VIDEOCONFERENCING . . . GIGABYTE . . . MODEM . . . MOUSE.

EVEN IF THESE PHRASES AREN'T A PART OF YOUR EVERY-DAY VOCABULARY, THEY ARE ALREADY MAKING AN IM-PACT ON YOUR LIFE. YOU MAY NOT REALIZE IT, BUT THE WORDS . . . AND THE CUTTING-EDGE TECHNOLOGY THEY DESCRIBE . . . ARE ACTUALLY A PART OF OUR WORLD RIGHT NOW.

WE LIVE IN AN EVER-INCREASING TECHNOLOGICAL WORLD, WHERE TECHNOLOGY TOUCHES EVERY FACET OF OUR EVERYDAY LIVES. FROM OUR HOME ENTERTAIN-MENT CENTERS, WITH THEIR REMOTE CONTROLS AND ENDLESS PROGRAMMING FEATURES . . . TO SOMETHING AS

ORDINARY AS BUYING GROCERIES AT THE SUPERMAR-
KET . . . TECHNOLOGY, AND MORE SPECIFICALLY, COM-
PUTER TECHNOLOGY . . . HAS TRANSFORMED THE WAY WE
LIVE, THE WAY WE VIEW OUR WORLD, AND YES, EVEN THE
WAY WE BANK.

Host/Narration

HELLO, I'M _____, AND I'LL BE YOUR HOST FOR THIS
COURSE ON LOTUS 1-2-3 RELEASE 5 FOR WINDOWS. THIS IS
THE INTERMEDIATE-LEVEL COURSE. YOU SHOULD HAVE AL-
READY TAKEN THE COMPANION COURSE, 1-2-3 RELEASE 5
BASICS, OR YOU SHOULD UNDERSTAND WORKSHEET FUN-
DAMENTALS LIKE COLUMNS, ROWS, CELLS, FORMULAS,
AND @ ["at"] FUNCTIONS. IN THIS COURSE WE'LL INTRO-
DUCE SOME OF THE MORE INTERESTING 1-2-3 FEATURES,
SUCH AS MULTIPLE WORKSHEETS, CHARTS AND GRAPH-
ICS, DATABASES, AND MACROS. THE COURSE IS DIVIDED
INTO 4 LESSONS AND INCLUDES A WORKBOOK THAT
YOU'LL USE WITH THE REAL 1-2-3 SOFTWARE TO PRACTICE
THE CONCEPTS THAT I'LL BE SHOWING YOU. SINCE THIS IS
A SELF-PACED COURSE, YOUR TIME WILL VARY, BUT COUNT
ON ABOUT A HALF DAY TO COMPLETE IT. IF YOU'RE READY,
LET'S GET STARTED.

Host/Narration

MOST OF US ARE FAMILIAR WITH THE IMAGE OF A JURY DE-
LIVERING A VERDICT. WE'VE SEEN IT ON TV SHOWS AND
LEARNED ABOUT JURIES IN CIVICS LESSONS. IN THE NEXT
FEW DAYS, YOU MAY BE DELIVERING A VERDICT IN A
UNITED STATES DISTRICT COURT.

SERVING AS A JUROR IS ONE OF THE MOST IMPORTANT
RESPONSIBILITIES YOU HAVE AS A CITIZEN OF THIS COUN-
TRY. THAT'S WHY WE'D LIKE TO TAKE A FEW MINUTES TO
TELL YOU ABOUT YOUR ROLE AS A JUROR AND GIVE YOU A
GENERAL IDEA OF WHAT TO EXPECT. ALONG THE WAY,
WE'LL HEAR FROM SOME PEOPLE WHO HAVE ALREADY
SERVED, AND GIVE YOU SOME DOS AND DON'TS ABOUT

BEING A JUROR. SHOULD YOU BE SELECTED TO SERVE ON A JURY, THE JUDGE IN THE CASE WILL TELL YOU MORE SPECIFICALLY WHAT YOU CAN AND CANNOT DO. BE SURE TO ASK IF YOU HAVE ANY QUESTIONS.

Interview with "Store Employee" (Antitheft Video)

AS A DETECTIVE FOR ALLIED, I CAN BE ANYTHING . . . FROM A WINDOW WASHER TO A BUM ON THE STREET . . . AND IN ONE PARTICULAR CASE, I WAS JUST THAT. WE SUSPECTED A GROUP OF STAFFERS OF STEALING MERCHANDISE FROM THE BACK OF THE STORE . . . THEY WERE WORKING AT NIGHT, AND WE DIDN'T WANT TO TAKE A CHANCE OF NOT GETTING CONCLUSIVE ENOUGH EVIDENCE ON CAMERA. SO, I WENT IN UNDER COVER . . . AS A BUM. I SAT RIGHT THERE AND WATCHED THE WHOLE OPERATION GO DOWN. NO ONE SUSPECTED A THING.

NO, I DON'T LIKE TURNING PEOPLE IN, BUT THESE PEOPLE ARE NOT WORKING FOR ALLIED. THEY'RE WORKING AGAINST ALLIED, AND AGAINST EVERY OTHER ALLIED STAFFER. WHEN I REMIND MYSELF OF THAT, I DON'T FEEL SO BAD.

In-House "News" Video

WELCOME TO THE PREMIER EDITION OF "CAPITAL FIRST," YOUR EYE ON WHAT'S HAPPENING THROUGHOUT C.S.I.

I'M _____. THIS MONTH WE'LL LOOK AT SOME OF THE EXCITING CHANGES ANNOUNCED AT LAUNCHES IN SCOTTSDALE AND ORLANDO . . . GET THE LATEST NEWS FROM CAPITAL SERVICES' ONLINE FEATURES . . . AND VISIT RICK THOMAS, VICE PRESIDENT OF MARKETING AND AD-VERTISING, FOR AN INSIDE LOOK AT UPCOMING TRENDS IN THE MARKETPLACE.

BUT FIRST, LET'S GO TO OUR FEATURE STORY, "BRAVE NEW WORLD," WHERE WE'LL HEAR FROM SOME OF THE EX-PERTS ON WHERE THE INDUSTRY IS HEADED AND WHERE C.S.I. FITS IN.

Human Resources Video

(These are often "right way, wrong way" scripts. Try this one with a good attitude, then a bad attitude.)

INTERVIEWER

THANKS FOR COMING IN TODAY. I REALIZE YOU MUST HAVE A VERY BUSY SCHEDULE.

INTERVIEWEE

NOT AT ALL. I APPRECIATE YOUR SEEING ME. I REALLY WANTED AN OPPORTUNITY TO TELL YOU IN PERSON HOW MUCH I WOULD LIKE TO WORK WITH YOU.

INTERVIEWER

GREAT. I HOPE WE CAN WORK IT OUT. NOW, I SEE FROM YOUR RÉSUMÉ THAT YOU HAVE HAD A GOOD DEAL OF EX-PERIENCE IN SALES AND MARKETING.

INTERVIEWEE

WELL, I WOULDN'T WANT TO OVERSTATE IT. I TOOK SEV-ERAL COURSES IN COLLEGE, AND I HAD A COUPLE OF SALES JOBS TO PAY PART OF MY TUITION. I'VE ALSO DONE SOME TELEMARKETING.

INTERVIEWER

WELL, LET'S BE FRANK, SOMETIMES IN BUSINESS, YOU FIND YOURSELF HAVING TO "SELL" SOMETHING THAT YOU MAY NOT BELIEVE IN 100 PERCENT. HOW ARE YOU IN THOSE CONDITIONS?

INTERVIEWEE

I DO PRETTY WELL. I'VE HAD TO SELL SOME THINGS I WASN'T TOTALLY COMMITTED TO.

THAT'S GOOD. IT MAY NOT BE OUR FAVORITE EXPERIENCE, BUT IN SOME WAYS WE CAN BENEFIT FROM IT IN THE LONG RUN.

Sales Training

CONSULTANT

THANKS FOR MEETING WITH ME. AS I EXPLAINED ON THE PHONE, AT WILSON/SHERMAN WE USE A PROCESS WE CALL *CLIENT-TALK* TO HELP US DEFINE OUR CLIENTS' EXPECTATIONS. WITH EXISTING CLIENTS, WE CONDUCT *CLIENT-TALK* INTERVIEWS AT LEAST ONCE A YEAR. WITH PROSPECTIVE CLIENTS LIKE YOURSELF, WE LIKE TO CONDUCT A *CLIENT-TALK* INTERVIEW BEFORE WE SUBMIT OUR PROPOSAL. IT HELPS US MAKE SURE WE UNDERSTAND WHAT THE CLIENT EXPECTS FROM US. AND IT ALSO GIVES THE POTENTIAL CLIENT A CHANCE TO "KICK OUR TIRES," SO TO SPEAK.

CLIENT

I THINK IT'S A GOOD IDEA. IN THE PAST, I'VE WORKED WITH CONSULTANTS WHO NEVER DID UNDERSTAND WHAT WE EXPECTED. FOR SOME OF THEM, IT WAS THE OLD ADAGE . . . THEIR ONLY TOOL WAS A HAMMER, SO EVERY PROBLEM WAS A NAIL!

CONSULTANT

HOPEFULLY, YOU'LL FIND THAT WE KNOW HOW TO LISTEN AND HOW TO RESPOND WITH MORE THAN JUST ONE IDEA. THIS PROJECT INVOLVES REENGINEERING YOUR COMPANY'S HUMAN RESOURCES FUNCTION. WHAT DO YOU EXPECT FROM THE CONSULTING FIRM YOU SELECT?

CLIENT

AN EXPERIENCED TEAM . . . PEOPLE WHO HAVE BEEN
THROUGH H-R REENGINEERING SEVERAL TIMES. STRONG
PROJECT LEADERSHIP AND MANAGEMENT SKILLS . . . STAY-
ING ON SCHEDULE, AND STAYING ON BUDGET. I HATE
BILLING SURPRISES!

MOST CLIENTS PROBABLY WOULDN'T SAY THIS, BUT I
WILL. CHEMISTRY IS IMPORTANT. THIS PROJECT WILL LAST
SIX MONTHS. IT'S IMPORTANT FOR ME TO LIKE YOUR TEAM
OF PEOPLE. I HAVE TO FEEL THESE GUYS WILL BE FUN TO
WORK WITH.

ONE FINAL THING I SHOULD ADD . . . AND IT'S AN EXPEC-
TATION THAT CONSULTANTS OFTEN FAIL TO MEET. DO
YOUR HOMEWORK. TAKE SOME TIME BEFORE THE PRESEN-
TATION TO LEARN ABOUT OUR COMPANY AND OUR BUSI-
NESS. THERE IS NOTHING THAT TURNS ME OFF FASTER
THAN SOME CONSULTANT WHO COMES IN, PLUNKS DOWN
A BIG BUDGET PROPOSAL, BUT DOESN'T KNOW HOW THIS
COMPANY MAKES MONEY, WHAT ISSUES DRIVE OUR INDUS-
TRY, WHO ARE OUR COMPETITORS . . . YOU GET THE PIC-
TURE?

Employee Training

FRANK *(Driving)*

WE'LL BE TALKING TO DAN WHITNEY. HE'S THE MANAGER
OF THE DIVISION THAT'S DEVELOPING THE DATA PROCESS-
ING SOFTWARE. THEY NEED ACTUAL TAX RETURNS AND
OTHER DOCUMENTS FOR THEIR COMPUTER PROGRAM-
MING PROTOTYPES.

JANET *(Passenger)*

DAN WHITNEY . . . WHAT'S HE LIKE?

FRANK

YOUNG, INTENSE, BRIGHT . . . HE NEEDS TO BE. MANAGE-MENT GAVE HIM A TOUGH JOB, OVERSEEING THE COM-PANY'S FIRST GOVERNMENT CONTRACT.

JANET

DOES SOUND LIKE A CHALLENGE . . . DOING THE STARTUP, AND NONE OF THE EMPLOYEES HAVE *SAFEDATA* TRAINING YET. THERE'S POTENTIAL FOR A LOT OF DISCLOSURES.

FRANK

(A look) . . . IF WE DO OUR JOB, THAT WON'T HAPPEN.

Consumer Information Video

SHE

WHEN WE BOUGHT THIS HOUSE, AND FOUND OUT IT HAD A HEAT PUMP, WE DIDN'T KNOW WHAT TO EXPECT.

HE

THE HOUSES WHERE WE GREW UP . . . EVEN OUR FIRST HOUSE TOGETHER . . . HAD THE MORE TRADITIONAL HEAT-ING SYSTEMS, SO WE WEREN'T FAMILIAR WITH HEAT PUMPS.

SHE

OUR REALTOR TOLD US THAT HEAT PUMP TECHNOLOGY IS ABOUT 30 YEARS OLD . . . AND THAT IT'S MORE EFFICIENT THAN CONVENTIONAL SYSTEMS. SINCE THE HEAT PUMP IS ALSO AN AIR-CONDITIONING SYSTEM, IT MAKES US COM-FORTABLE ALL YEAR.

HE

WHAT I LIKE IS THAT IT'S CLEAN . . . AND THERE ARE NO PROBLEMS WITH DELIVERY OR THE TANK RUNNING DRY, LIKE WE HAD LAST WINTER AT THE OTHER HOUSE.

SHE

DESPITE ALL THAT, WE STILL DIDN'T KNOW EXACTLY HOW IT WORKED . . . OR WHAT WE HAD TO DO TO MAINTAIN IT.

Appendix B
MOS *Exercises*

The point of these exercises is to tell a story without the benefit of dialogue. The "audience" should have a sense of where you are, who you are, what your state of mind is, and whether someone else is in your story. You need to imagine your environment in great detail so that your mind and body can react naturally to the environment that you "see" in your story.

Putting another person in your improvisation offers much greater potential for storytelling and reactions. It also opens you up to the camera, since you can use the camera as the "other person."

You don't need to be silent, you just need to tell a story without being a script writer. However, by all means, keep a "script" running constantly in your mind. Your body will then be able to act out that *inner dialogue*.

What makes these stories interesting is the detail. For instance, if you are in a restaurant and are served a meal, you don't just start "eating." Just like in real life, you look at the meal, tell yourself how it looks, push the plate around, maybe smell the sauce first. You do all that before you even pick up your imaginary fork.

As for props, you can use simple things such as a hat or a pencil, but improvisations should not be about props. At an audition that involved tasting, you might be given a plastic fork or spoon, but otherwise your props would be limited to what you had in your pockets or purse.

Working on your improvisation skills not only prepares you for when you have an improvisation audition, but it also improves the auditions where you have dialogue, because it gets you in the habit of using internal dialogue to fill out the story you are telling.

Keep in mind that you are not trying to be funny or entertaining when you do an improvisation; you are trying to tell a story. You will find that you often want to end your improvisation with a physical "punch line." There does need to be a sense of when your improvisation is finished, so some kind of physical "period" does accomplish that very well. You should not just shrug your shoulders with a "Well, that's all I have." Doing that has the effect of making a negative comment on your improvisation. If you don't have an "ending," just break your focus, look at the camera, and smile or nod.

Also keep in mind — and this is true of any acting you do — that *passive choices are almost always less interesting than active choices*. So, for instance, if you look out a window, don't just look out the window, but see something and have an opinion about what you see. If you sit in a car, don't just sit in the car, but sink into the seat and have an opinion about how the leather feels and smells.

MOS Exercise #1

This one does have one line, just to help you put a tag on the story.

> YOU WALK UP TO A CAR (use a chair), GET IN, LOOK AROUND, AND END BY SAYING, "BUICK, YOU'RE MY KIND OF CAR!"

We need to get a sense of where you are, how you feel, and so on. For instance, you might be in a showroom, or on the street. This might be your car, or you might be a car thief. You might be having a great day or a terrible day. Think of what you do when you get in a car — the buttons you fondle, the things you adjust.

Cram your story full of detail. You want the improvisation to last about thirty seconds, but don't worry about the time — just tell a rich story.

MOS Exercise #2

> YOU ARE IN A RESTAURANT. YOU TAKE A BITE OF FOOD. *IT TASTES TERRIBLE!* YOU WANT TO GET IT OUT OF YOUR MOUTH WITHOUT ANYONE NOTICING.

Because you don't want others to notice, and also because TV commercials are overwhelmingly positive, your task is to always look pleasant. In this case, that will also give you the greatest opportunity for humor.

This improvisation, especially, invites you to put other people into your story. The waiter, your dining partner, and people walking by all give you someone to react to, and a way to stay alive and in contact with the camera.

The moment people often fail to fill out in this story is the two or three seconds of "realization" that happen between the time you take the bite and you taste how bad the bite really is.

MOS *Exercise #3*

This could be your audition for a lottery commercial, and it is an excellent exercise for practicing a broad range of expression. Of course, because it's a TV commercial, and not real life, even an expression of disappointment would be pleasant. So, instead of playing "Damn!" you play, "Well, what are you gonna do?" Your one scripted word is "Thanks," which you say to your imaginary ticket seller. Beyond that, you can make whatever noises you want. They get pretty excited on some of those commercials.

> YOU STEP UP TO A COUNTER TO BUY A LOTTERY TICKET. YOU SCRATCH IT OFF. IT SAYS $0. YOU REACT, AND SAY, "THANKS." YOU DECIDE TO TAKE A SECOND ONE, WHICH YOU SCRATCH AND FIND $10. YOU REACT, AND SAY, "THANKS." YOU TAKE A THIRD TICKET, WHICH YOU SCRATCH OFF AND FIND YOU HAVE WON $100,000. YOU RE-ACT, AND SAY, "THANKS!"

The most interesting parts of this story are when you go through your decisions to buy another ticket, how you feel about the results, and your progression of emotion. The most common mistake with this exercise is spending a long time on the scratching of the ticket, or bending over so we are only looking at the top of your head. Unless you scratch your ticket in some interesting way to enhance your characterization, you should move quickly through that part. It is emotionally passive, and your story stops while you are doing it.

MOS *Exercise #4*

This is a variation on commercials you see every year, inviting you to leave winter behind and come to some wildly fun, sun-drenched location. As an exercise, we invite you to "let your hair down" and be as uninhibited as TV would allow.

YOU JUST GOT ON THE BUS TO RIDE TO WORK, WET AND COLD FROM THE RAIN. YOU TAKE A SEAT (OR NOT), AND BEGIN TO DREAM ABOUT ESCAPING TO SOME ISLAND RESORT.

The goals here are broad ranges of emotion (misery to joy), and free expression. In the commercial, your wild imaginings might take place in a "bubble" over your head, but for the audition, you would do it live. Don't let your daydream get passive. Take us with you. If you are dreaming of music, let yourself start singing or dancing. You could tee off a golf ball, or start disrobing to lather yourself up with sunscreen, or offer the imaginary person next to you a drink. The obvious tag for this is coming back to reality, with the help of the imaginary people around you. Mainly, have a lot of fun.

Appendix C
Resource Reading List

Ross Reports-TV. Television Index Inc., 1515 Broadway, New York, NY 10109-0025.
Available at theatre outlets. Published monthly with updated lists of casting directors, agents, network primetime programs, daytime serials, network producers, and more.

Backstage. 1515 Broadway, 14th Floor, New York, NY 10036 and 5055 Wilshire Blvd., Los Angeles, CA 90036.
A weekly trade periodical published on both coasts, with extensive listings of auditions in theatre and film, both union and nonunion.

The Actor's Picture/Résumé Book by Jill Charles and Tom Bloom (1991). Dorset, VT: Theatre Directories/American Theatre Works, Inc.
An excellent guide.

The Artist's Way: A Spiritual Path to Higher Creativity by Julia Cameron and Mark Bryan (1995). New York: J. P. Tarcher.
For writers, poets, painters, musicians—and creative people from all walks of life.

Daily Word: Silent Unity's Magazine. 1901 NW Blue Parkway, Unity Village, MO 64065-0001. http://www.dailyword.org.
A nondenominational guide for daily encouragement and spiritual nutrition.

Acting in Television Commercials for Fun and Profit by Squire Fridell (1995). New York: Crown.
A swell book, somewhat oriented to the West Coast.

Acting in Commercials: A Guide to Auditioning and Performing on Camera (2d ed.) by Joan See (1988). Lakewood, NJ: Watson-Guptill. Excellent advanced training, especially for students of the Meisner technique.

Audition by Michael Shurtleff (1980). New York: Bantam. Superb!

Appendix D
Headshot Pre-Session Information

Any photographer you choose to work with for a headshot will discuss with you their ideas for wardrobe, and will give you basic information on how they work. **Elizabeth Lehmann,** the New York-based photographer with whom Brenna works exclusively for her headshots (and whom she highly recommends), was kind enough to provide us with a copy of the information sheet that she gives to clients, allowing us to pass on an excerpt. This very useful information will also give you an idea of what to expect, and what is expected from an excellent photographer.

Clothing

For each of the particular markets you're interested in, study those markets, look for your type, and note the kinds of roles played, as well as styles of clothing worn. Based on your observations, how would you tend to be cast for commercials, soaps, other TV programming, film, theatre, or industrials? Let this guide the styles of clothing you select for your session. As well as style, keep in mind tone and texture.

In general, bring shirts/blouses that are lighter or darker than your skin tone. What reads the same tone as Caucasian skin tone, for example, is sweatshirt grey, khaki, salmon, turquoise, hot pink, and therefore these are not desirable unless layered with a contrasting tone. You want to go lighter—like pastels—or darker—from the primary colors to purple, hunter green, rust, garnet, even to black. The goal is to have tone separation between your skin, clothing, and hair.

Clothes with texture are better than those without. For example: a cotton-knit sweater is better than a flat cotton shirt. Angora wool, silk, leather, denim, tweed, cotton knit, satin, crushed velvet, and suede are several fabrics that have good texture.

Avoid contrasty prints and bold patterns. Clothes that have shape to them are better than the baggy look. Extra fabric adds extra pounds. Because we're including more body shots these days, bottoms do matter. Darker colors are better because they make you look slimmer. So bring jeans, slacks, leggings, and skirts to go with your tops accordingly.

Overall, think in terms of bringing clothes that are casual but put together, and some clothes that are dressier and more upscale. In particular, think about the specific markets you're interested in, and how many different shots you want. Good casual looks (commercials, musical theatre, TV sitcoms): The Gap, J. Crew, L. L. Bean, Tweeds. Good upscale looks (theatre, film, TV drama, industrials): GQ, Details, Victoria's Secret, Ann Taylor, Saks.

Music for Session

Feel free to bring any of your favorite cassette tapes or CDs to play during your session. Otherwise you may choose from my repertoire of music.

Inner Preparations

Given that there are no technical problems, what people respond to in a photograph is life, spontaneity, and truthfulness. I try to capture the feeling of a caught moment throughout the session. There are several ways to do this. One is by interacting with you as you're looking into the camera. Another is having you look away and into the camera repeatedly, as if you just caught someone's eye.

Many people find it helpful to prepare monologues, stories, or fantasies beforehand, that they deliver/tell through their eyes during the session. It's like rolling a movie through your head.

Try to select material that makes you laugh, conveys strength, shows warmth and caring, is flirtatious and is playful (not necessarily all in one piece). You can also bring music that elicits these responses in you.

You can practice this at home. Think of saying the monologue, story, or fantasy through your eyes while looking in the mirror, projecting the energy outward. Allow yourself to go with it, rather than judge and inhibit yourself.

Care for Yourself

The week before your session try to drink a lot of water, keep alcohol consumption low, get enough sleep each night, and stay out of the sun. If you plan to get your hair cut or processed, do so at least a week before the session, to let it settle in. The day of your session don't arrive on an empty stomach. Allow ample time to arrive punctually, not feeling stressed out.

Appendix E
Union Offices

This is the current list of Screen Actors Guild (SAG) offices (the primary union for commercials and films). In many cases, they share or can direct you to the local AFTRA (American Federation of Television and Radio Artists) office if you are interested.

SAG's Web site is www.sag.com.

National Office
5757 Wilshire Boulevard
Los Angeles, CA 90036
(213) 954-1600

Arizona
1616 E. Indian School Road
Suite 330
Phoenix, AZ 85016
(602) 265-2712

Atlanta
455 E. Paces Ferry Road N.E.
Suite 334
Atlanta, GA 30305
(404) 239-0131

Boston
11 Beacon Street
Room 512
Boston, MA 02108
(617) 742-2688

Chicago
75 E. Wacker Drive
14th Floor
Chicago, IL 60601
(312) 372-8081

**Colorado, Nevada,
New Mexico, Utah**
950 S. Cherry Street
Suite 502
Denver, CO 80222
(303) 757-6226

Dallas-Ft. Worth
6060 N. Central Expressway
Suite 302, LB 604
Dallas, TX 75206
(214) 363-8300

Detroit
28690 Southfield Road
#290 A & B
Lathrup Village, MI 48076
(810) 559-9540

Florida
7300 N. Kendell Drive
Suite 620
Miami, FL 33156
(305) 670-7677

Central Florida
Sun Bank Plaza
3393 West Vine Street #302
Kissimmee, FL 34741
(407) 847-4445

Hawaii
949 Kapiolani Boulevard
Suite 105
Honolulu, HI 96814
(808) 596-0138

Houston
2650 Fountainview Drive
Suite 326
Houston, TX 77057
(713) 972-1806

Nashville
1108 17th Avenue So.
Nashville, TN 37212
(615) 327-2944

New York
1515 Broadway
44th Floor
New York, NY 10036
(212) 944-1030

Philadelphia
230 S. Broad Street
5th Floor
Philadelphia, PA 19102
(215) 545-3150

San Diego
7827 Convoy Court
Suite 400
San Diego, CA 92111
(619) 278-7695

San Francisco
235 Pine Street
11th Floor
San Francisco, CA 94104
(415) 391-7510

Washington, D.C.
4340 East West Highway
Suite 204
Bethesda, MD 20814
(301) 657-2560

Appendix F
Glossary

AD: Assistant director. Employed on larger-scale shoots mostly, this person will give you most of your direction and information, and will be your liaison with the actual director.

Booking: A specific offer of employment, which once verbally accepted by you or by your agent, represents a binding commitment.

Camera left: Directions are given from the point of view of the camera. This is the camera's left—your right as you face the camera.

Camera right: Directions are given from the point of view of the camera. This is the camera's right—your left as you face the camera.

Chromakey: The performer works in front of a colored screen, usually blue or green. In postproduction, the screen is replaced with video images.

Class A Spot: A spot that airs on network programming during primetime to a national audience. The actor receives the largest residual payments for this type of use.

CU: Close-up. Just the face, or the face and neck, are in view of the camera.

Cut, or **cutaway:** An instantaneous change from one scene to another.

Director: The person in charge at the shooting of the commercial or film. The director is sometimes the photographer also, and might own the equipment.

Dissolve: One scene fades out as another fades in.

Downstage: Closer to the camera or audience.

DVE: Digital video effects. Computer-generated effects, used in editing, such as wipes, page turns, zooms, and thousands of others.

ECU: Extreme close-up. A shot mostly of the eyes.

First Refusal, or **Hold:** Terms used (and abused) to indicate a producer's interest in employing an actor for a project. The use of these terms varies from market to market, and it can be argued that neither term obligates anyone to anything. Rather, they are a courtesy extended by the actor, where the actor promises not to accept any other employment without first being released by the producer "holding" that time. You might have a first, a second, and even a third refusal for the same day. But, if someone wants to book you, the producer to whom you gave a refusal must either release you or book you themselves.

Gaffer: The crew chief, responsible for the equipment, who usually sets the lights for a shot.

Grip: A crew person who is the equivalent of a stagehand in theatre.

Hitting the mark: This has to do with the actor's ability to move to and stop at a specific place (which is usually indicated by tape on the floor), or to place a product in the exact location the director wants, whether on a surface or in mid-air.

Holding fee: For actors working under a union contract, this is a fee paid to the actor for each thirteen-week cycle that the client "holds" the spot for use, and is usually equal to the original session fee. In return, the actor is obligated not to do a commercial for any competing products.

Key light: The primary light on an actor or a scene.

LS: Long shot. Farther back, perhaps at a distance.

Master shot: A single shot of a scene, from beginning to end, photographed fairly wide, which is later edited together with the close-ups, OTSs, etc. If a director shoots a master shot, then the actors need to remember and match their actions as closely as possible when the close-ups, OTSs, and reverses are shot.

MOS: A scene in which the sound is not recorded. Perhaps it stands for "mitt out sound" or "minus optical strip."

MS: Medium shot. Framed perhaps to the waist.

OTS: Over the shoulder. A shot looking at the face of one actor, photographed from behind another actor and framed with a bit of the second actor's head, neck, and/or shoulder in view. Usually alternates with the reverse shot over the shoulder of the first actor.

PA: Production assistant. A "does everything" person attached to the production, but not on the film crew.

PSA: Public service announcement. Commercials produced by the government or advocacy groups that are meant to inform the public about a product or cause, or to raise awareness about an issue affecting public health, such as drugs, lead paint, or the use of seat belts.

Residuals: Fees paid for "usage," the rerunning of a commercial (or film or TV show) in which the actor appears as a principal actor. Fees are based on the number of times the commercial airs and the size of the audience who might see it.

Room tone: A short recording of the ambient sound of a room or area. It is needed for editing purposes, and is usually recorded in each location by turning on the actor's microphone and having everyone stand completely still.

Session fee: The fee you are paid for a day's work on a commercial. If you are not a celebrity, your fee will probably be at scale, an amount that has been negotiated by the unions.

Slate: At an audition, the spoken self-introduction by an actor at the beginning of his or her take. A "video handshake." On the shoot, a spoken or written identification before each take of a scene.

Split screen: Two or more scenes showing on screen at the same time.

Spot: The commonly used term for a commercial.

Super: Graphics that are later superimposed over the picture.

Take: The recorded performance of a scene or moment.

Two-Shot: A shot of two people in a scene.

Upstage: On a set, farther away from the camera or audience.

VO: Voice-over. Recorded separately, just the voice of an actor heard over a scene or video footage.

Wild spot: A commercial that airs on an independent or nonnetwork station, or that airs on a regular network station but between the commercials provided with the network programming. "Wild spotting" allows the sponsor to target local markets or specific demographics that offer the greatest potential for selling the product.